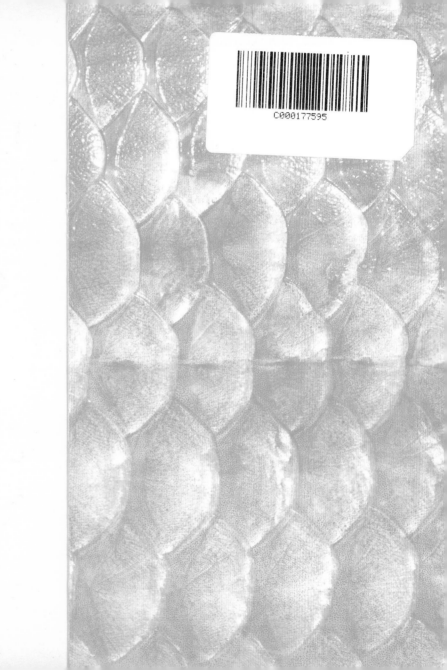

About the Author

Chris Yates was born in Epsom in 1948 a
first carp five years later, after which his life r
orbited this fish up to the date of the diary in
   He now lives near Salisbury in Wiltshi
some exquisite carp ponds, but probably sp
time on the rivers nowadays (when he's not
to be an author and a photographer).

THE LOST DIARY

April–September 1981

Fishing Diary

of

C. Fernyhough Yates

unbound

This edition first published in 2013

Unbound
4–7 Manchester Street, Marylebone, London, W1U 2AE
www.unbound.co.uk

Typeset by Bracketpress
Cover design by Mecob

A CIP record for this book is available from the British Library

ISBN 978-1-78352-043-5 (Trade)
ISBN 978-1-78352-042-8 (Ebook)
ISBN 978-1-78352-044-2 (Ltd Edn)

Printed in England by Clays Ltd, Bungay, Suffolk

PROLOGUE

This diary, which was lost for over twenty years and has recently been found again in a box of Christmas decorations, concerns not only my last season at Redmire Pool, but also the last season in which I fished almost exclusively for carp. It begins in the spring of 1981 and ends in the autumn, but amongst the many lovely days by the waterside there is never an actual moment that seems to mark the beginning of any diminishing enthusiasm for what was then my favourite species. Rather, it appears from the writing that my devotion to the golden scales becomes deeper as the diary progresses, so maybe the clues lie elsewhere.

Since the age of five, when I saw a seemingly miraculous creature in my local village pond and learned that it was a carp, I had been more or less obsessed by this fish. In June 1980, when I was thirty-two and had just caught what was then the largest British carp ever, I wondered if my obsession had been cured. But then I had a mad idea that, having landed a fifty-pounder, I could now dream of capturing Redmire's real monster, the King, a fish I'd glimpsed only once, yet knew was possibly the biggest carp in Europe.

Like all anglers, I'm always hoping that an outsize fish will take my bait, but I have never narrowed my vision to the exclusion of the more easily attainable angling delights. Indeed, I have always felt that a single-minded Captain Ahab quest for an individual monster is a sign of a slightly psychotic or maybe rather boring personality. Yet, by June '81, while I had not lost my enthusiasm for *any* size of carp, there was this curious thought that, having gifted me once with a colossus, maybe Redmire would be generous again. Certainly, as you will discover, I came very close to another of the pool's aristocarp, but it wasn't in the way I'd imagined; and as the days and weeks passed I began to sense that Redmire was not just telling me that I must never take her for granted, she was also teaching me a sobering lesson.

Maybe it was this that, eventually, marked a change in my angling outlook, or perhaps it was the effect of a troubling pettiness in the governance of the actual ten-man Redmire syndicate that I allude to in the early pages. However, whatever it was, it didn't spoil my enjoyment of what was another magical if sometimes challenging season. And as well as the fishing there were discoveries of new waters, nostalgic pilgrimages to old haunts, meetings with new friends and occasional unexpected encounters with creatures other than fish and with presences that were not quite human.

The actual writing was done either in quiet moments

on the bank – and there were plenty of those – or at home, which was, in the 1980s, Vale Cottage, a lovely old barn of a cottage in a wooded valley – Whitmore Vale – on the Hampshire/Surrey border. And, of course, I always used my old 1930s Swan fountain pen.

Christopher Yates
Cranbourne Chase
Autumn, 2013

APRIL

Thursday 9th

It was hot – hotter than it had been last June – and, as Clare and I drove down to Guildford, I couldn't understand why I was wearing such a heavy pullover. She was going to the record shop; I went to Jefferies to have a look at their small collection of centre-pins. There was nothing that felt just right in my hands, but they did have a very nice old creel for only six pounds, which I bought instead. And then, as I was walking down the street to meet Clare, a shining golden carp almost leapt out at me from the window of the brass knick-knack shop. So I had to buy that as well. The vision of it inspired me to seek out the real thing, and the unexpectedly summery weather gave me hope of success. So, on the way home, I cunningly suggested that we glug down the chilled ginger beer we'd just bought on the banks of Forked Pond.

Blimey! The carp were obviously just waiting for us. I had no idea the water was so well populated, though, obviously, being the close season, the fish were far more visible than they will be in June. I climbed an oak tree and watched as several beautiful creatures cruised past beneath me, mirrors and commons, some well over

25lbs. In all, there must have been about thirty fish enjoying the sunshine, though most were in the 10–12lbs range. Lovely to see them – and as they serenely drifted below me I remembered the half-dream from last night when, just as I was dipping towards sleep, I glimpsed the ghostly image of a deep swimming carp in a deeply blue lake.

Tuesday 14th

It rained and the wind was cool from the north-east. Began rewriting my June article, 'The Prospect of Dawn', for *Angling*, sorry that the magazine was about to change its name to the far less appealing *Coarse Fishing Monthly* (I shall continue to refer to it in here by its original title). The sun came out at mid-morning so I moved into the garden, where the writing suddenly took a new, unexpected and favourable direction.

In the afternoon I took a break and went down to see Donald Leney at Springhead. We had tea in his study, enjoying a widely ranging conversation, though perhaps 'widely ranging' is the wrong term as we were only concerned with a hundred aspects of water life (carp, golden tench, Redmire, trout, pondweed, dragonflies etc.). Leney had gathered a few of his favourite books for me to borrow: *With Nets and Lines* by T. A. Waterhouse, *Wood Pool* by BB and *The Fisherman's Fireside Book*, an interesting-looking anthology that I'd not heard of before. In return, I gave him a copy of this month's *Angling* with the group portrait of the Golden Scale Club. He was quite impressed. 'This fellow, bottom left,' he said, having recognised me, 'is the one who looks best the part.' And he laughed. Then Mrs Packham came in with another tray of her just-baked slab cake and a fresh pot of tea; and by the time I left, the moon was rising, white, behind the silhouette of the dead wellingtonia in Leney's garden.

Now I'm probably not going to finish the article before my dear editor's deadline. Sorry, Sandy, but some things have to take precedence over other things.

Thursday 16th

Left for Redmire at 6.00pm and was in Ross-on-Wye at 9.10. I got some fish and chips there, and then went on to Langarren to phone Clare and inform her of my safe arrival. Finally, I rolled down the grassy slope to the pool, stepping out into the moonlight and taking in a deep draught of Redmire's sweet air (exactly a month before the new season starts and the balsam poplar leaves must just now be unfurling). But the night is far colder than I anticipated and I've only got my lightweight sleeping bag.

Friday 17th

A cold wind rippled the pool at dawn, but the sky was clear and it was lovely to see Redmire in the first green flush of spring. However, I didn't have much time to appreciate the morning or sneak along the banks looking for signs of carp. In fact I'd only just boiled a kettle for tea when I heard the drone of an approaching car. It was Barry's, and within the hour we were joined by Ron, Henry, John, Dave, Steve and Tom, all eager to finish the work on the dam repair that we'd begun last month. And after that we spent the rest of the day trimming the thorns, clipping the willows and felling and sawing the last of the dead elms.

When we'd finally packed away our tools we made a big pot of tea and gathered on the dam to watch the sunlight fading on the pool. When I went up to the ash tree on Greenbanks to get my stuff from last night I heard a lapwing. It was swooping over the ploughed field on my right, the rounded wings flashing in the sunset. The moon had just appeared, a day before full, and the bird

4

swept right across its yellow face, then dived, soared upward and looped sideways, all the while uttering its high clear call, as if celebrating its special place between rising moon and setting sun.

We all went into Ross where we had supper in a rather dispiriting pub and talked rather too seriously about plans for the coming season. I drove home through the moonlight, on 'empty' for the forty-two miles after Newbury. My wife-warmed bed was delightful after the rigours of the day and the cold discomfort of last night.

Tuesday 28th

After Clare had made an early tea of home-baked crumpets and fruit cake, I set off along a winding road that led due east across Sussex. The landscape was grey but mostly lovely; the traffic was almost non-existent and the farms and villages seemed deserted.

I was going to meet Lawrence Breakspeare, who'd written last month, telling me that, because I'd outwitted the 'technocrats of modern carp fishing' by catching a record fish on vintage tackle, he'd now like to offer something as a token of appreciation. He didn't sound unhealthily earnest and I was sure he wasn't angling for an invite to Redmire or anything like that; he seemed, once we'd spoken on the phone, to be a genuine if slightly eccentric carp fisher. We arranged a time and place to meet, but I'd underestimated the distance and was nearly an hour late (at the Star at Heathfield). Someone was standing outside the pub, looking very bored, but he suddenly smiled as he recognised me and I knew it must be Lawrence. Of course I apologised and insisted I buy the first round, but he said no, he was only slightly furious about waiting and, anyway, the evening was at his expense.

We sat down at a table in a quiet bar and because it soon became obvious that he shared my attitudes to nearly all things fishy, it was like a meeting between two old friends. Lawrence said he was still chuckling because of my monster carp of last year and, as a form of congratulation, he handed me a new bamboo rod. It was a Walker's of Hythe Mk IV blank that he'd expertly finished himself and, in ink on the butt, christened the Bernithan Beauty.

What a man! But I felt a bit awkward accepting it. He'd gone to a lot of trouble over it and I didn't deserve it, because all I'd done was to catch an outsize fish. 'Yet there is something more,' he said. Inspired by my last article about the Golden Scale Club and its search for the ultimate carp pool, he went searching himself and discovered a hidden-away, unknown water. It contained fish of unknown size – carp, tench, rudd and trout. He'd already secured it and, if we liked, the club were welcome to share it with him.

'Now just hang on a minute,' I said. 'If you think that your admittedly generous offer is going to lead towards inevitable membership of such an exclusive brother-hood…then, welcome aboard.'

In good spirits, we were thrown out after closing time and agreed to meet again next month – on the banks of our new club water.

Y.A.M.

MAY

Thursday 7th

Came down late on a day that was grey and slow, but warm. Read a bit, wrote a bit, but didn't do any photography even though I have five book covers to deliver by next week. I watched clouds build up over the half-green woods and billow towards our cottage; then the rain began to pour. We couldn't go out for a walk and there wasn't even time for Clare to go out for a skip before tea. And, afterwards, at about 5.00pm, I waved her bye-bye as I set off again along the road to Sussex, heading to Lewes this time. I arrived at the town, suddenly forgetting whereabouts exactly I was meant to go. But then, by absurd luck, I spotted a familiar figure standing in the rain by a small car park. It was Lawrence. I transferred from my van to his car and we drove through rain, thunder and lightning to a village under the South Downs. Turning down a narrow track, we passed a farm, parked under a brick railway bridge and, ignoring the storm, walked alongside the railway until we came to an overhanging copse. Just visible through the trees was a sheet of dark deep-looking water and after scrambling down through a blackthorn thicket we were standing on the bankside of what is destined to become the Golden Scalers' own carp pool.

Reed-fringed, tree-shadowed, it had the authentic brooding atmosphere of a classic carp water. There was an island with willows, spreading beds of floating pondweed and dead skeletal trees half submerged in the margins. I made the carp fisher's challenge, as dreamed up by Lawrence, before setting off on a thorough exploration of the banks. We found a half-rotten barn door, probably the remains of a fishing platform, lying in a reed bed. It offered a good vantage point across the width of the pool and was still strong enough to bear our weight. Though the rain had, by then, stopped, the fading light denied us any chance of fish spotting, but there was another way of detecting the pool's inhabitants.

We stamped heavily on the old boards and, to our delight, several large ripples immediately spread out from the weedbeds. We stamped again and a massive bow wave bulged towards the far bank. The whole pool rocked like a swelling sea and the reflection of the new moon – the clouds miraculously parted just then – wobbled but didn't break.

A group of swifts came screaming in over the trees, the first of the year for me. A cuckoo called. The evening cleared and calmed, feeling suddenly like summer. Something was brewing.

When the light had almost gone, we walked back to the car and drove to the village pub, hoping it would befit the evening's atmosphere. It didn't. It was depressing. So we tried the next village and found a more welcoming place where we could sit in a dim-lit bar with our ale and burble about fish till closing time.

It was midnight when I got back to Whitmore Vale. Clare, already in bed, was glad to see me. But I said I was going to make a snack as I hadn't eaten anything all evening and the silly person insisted on coming down to make me a giant salad sandwich.

Thursday 14th

The joy of the close season lies, firstly, in the increase of time to do things other than fishing and, secondly, in the cooking up of dreams connected with fishing. And one of the best ways to cook up a fishing dream is simply to visit the waterside. Lake and river watching is always a pleasure, but in the close season it's more enchanting because you're looking at the water differently. Freed from the chore of fiddling about with fishing tackle, you can concentrate more fully on what's going on under the surface and, knowing the fish are in a haven of inaccessibility, just the vaguest glimpse of one can fire up all kinds of wild hopes for the coming season. And so you come home with a headful of dreams.

Today I wanted to revisit some of the places that used to inspire the dreams of my childhood and so I drove over to Brockham, meeting Henry on the green because he wanted to see some of these waters himself. After a pint in the Dukes Head we walked the quarter mile to the old field pond where, because we weren't carrying rods, the carp were very happy to show themselves. Why hadn't we brought a loaf of bread for them? Then we went over to the footbridge on the Mole and stared down into the clear water, hoping to spot a chub, but only seeing a shoal of minnows. The slow rhythmic swaying of the weed tresses in the current was too mesmerising to stare at for long. Next, we drove to Betchworth so that we could gaze again into the old lime pit, Woodhill, where I'd spent many happy and sometimes dramatic fishing days in the mid-Sixties. Apart from the sad scum of rubbish in some of the margins it hadn't changed at all. The deep water was as crystalline as ever and I bet the monster carp I used to chase are now true monsters. All we saw were the usual shoals of small colourful rudd and perch flitting between the weed-stems. We said we might have to return in June or July, before the school holidays start, and bring some of our almost adult experience to bear on what is still a special place. But I bet we never come back.

Henry wasn't aware of Buckland Court Pond, which I used to poach as a sixteen-year-old, but where, as with Woodhill, I never succeeded in catching a carp. We drove the two or three miles eastward only to discover it had completely dried up. It looked haunted and miserable, just a saucer-shaped bowl of finely crazed powdery mud. It was a sad place to say goodbye, but Henry had to head home then, while I wanted to continue with my nostalgic jaunt.

I drove down to Sussex to have a look at another old favourite, Titmus Lake, where I once hooked and lost a possible twenty-pounder in '68. It was the same as I remember from '76, when I last visited it, but not nearly as attractive as it used to be in the old days, before the local council began to make their hideous improvements.

Finally, I returned to the water of the moment, Pitchfords Pond (named after our potential new Vice President, BB). I made a quick cup of tea in the parking place under the railway bridge before walking across the field, over the stream and through the wood to the water.

Lawrence was already there, as I guessed he would be, and I joined him on the platform where he'd been watching for carp. Last time he'd visited he'd seen a beautiful double-figure common glide right past him. Today we only saw rudd, but some of them were quite large.

It was a warm evening and very pleasant just wandering round the banks, staring into the water, dreaming of what might be down there. But eventually we lost patience and stamped on the ground, like last time, causing a great commotion as some large unseen fish swirled heavily out by the island. It left a great black hole in the floating weed.

The sun set and we went for a pint. Lawrence said that, because he'd enjoyed the pieces I'd done for *Angling*, I should start writing a fishing book *'Right now!'*

'Fat chance,' I said. 'Too many other things to do.'

Friday 15th

A letter came from Biggles (now Algy) Selwood, which I refrained from opening until after Clare and I got back from the market. It was brilliant, fit for the G.S.C. archive. I shall have to arrange a meeting with him soon. Among the more ludicrous scribblings was a request for Lawrence to build him a new carp rod. Lawrence is soon going to have his time seriously compromised by his recent elevation to official G.S.C. rod-builder.

Did no work of any kind. Could not apply myself to any serious thought or occupation – except for my angling books, especially *Float and Fly*, a great little anthology lent by Lawrence – who must now be known only as Rollo as he doesn't want his name mentioned in print '…in case it spoils things.' (!) This makes me wonder whether he's working for M.I.6. or maybe the British Carp Study Group.

Monday 18th

It seemed to rain all day and I seemed to be on the phone all afternoon. It appears that I might have stirred up a hornet's nest simply because I agreed, with my old Redmire pal Rod (Hutchinson), to make an inaugural speech at the first meeting of a new national angling fraternity, the Carp Society. But because of a conflict of interests between some of the Redmire syndicate and members of this group, I have been advised by the syndicate that I should have nothing to do with them. Someone, it appears, has heard a rumour that the Society wants to mount a Redmire takeover. And so the phone has been hot because of various, mostly wobbly arguments and counter-arguments. I spoke to Rod who, like me, thinks the conspiracy idea is completely laughable. We only agreed to do the talk because we have lots of friends in the Society who just see it as a good excuse to meet up regularly and chat about the things we like doing best. Why should that seem so suspicious? I know Rod would like to fish Redmire again, but if he joins the Society he might undermine his chances. And if I join? Will I then have to fish Redmire under a cloud? Or perhaps I should simply leave the malcontents to themselves and walk away? This is silly. I don't want to spoil Redmire's atmosphere, or upset people, but no one should be clamped for consorting with their friends. So I shall write my no doubt very daft speech, have a good laugh with Rod about old times and blithely carry on with my plans for the new season. The weather will no doubt change next week and so hopefully we can all agree to fish together in peace.

Tuesday 19th

The dawn chorus began at 4.14. I was already awake when I heard the first bird – a melancholy robin; the blackbirds followed more tunefully, then the full choir. I was sleepless because I was still slightly troubled by thoughts of petty bickering between anglers. And then I thought a curious thought: 'This is my night, I have to get across it on my own – so bugger off you demons!' They vanished like shadows and, lulled by the birds, I fell back to sleep.

I was meant to be going up to Crazyland today to deliver a picture of a tidal wave to Sphere, but Rollo phoned after breakfast to say he couldn't visit tomorrow, as planned. Therefore, could he come today instead? Of course he could – apart from anything else it's always nice to have an excuse not to go to Crazyland. The tidal wave can wait till tomorrow.

An hour later, Ritchie Macdonald phoned, wanting to add his strongly worded contribution to the Redmire/ Carp Society debate. Dear Ritchie! I love his direct approach, but I told him not to take the issue so seriously. After all, it was only fishing. 'Only fishing!' he said, outraged. And I knew exactly how he felt, especially as it seems that, against his will, he might not be fishing Redmire this season. In the middle of the conversation, just as we began to chuckle at the absurdity of it all, Rollo arrived. I wished Ritchie well, put down the phone and went to make my visitor a cup of tea.

He obviously approved of our little hovel and its position in the middle of the woods. After the pot of tea, I walked him over to the Wells, taking a bag of bread for the carp. Rollo loved the look of the pool, but there was

not a fish in sight until he made his special carp fisher's
challenge.

'To all patriarchs and matriarchs dwelling in this
pond,' he intoned solemnly, 'I summon you now
to … blah-blah-blah etc., etc.'

It seemed to affect the carp like a clap of thunder!
The entire colony suddenly materialised on the surface,
cruising around in close formations, completely uncon-
cerned by our presence and slurping down every crust we
offered them. It was a pity we hadn't waited till the new
season before throwing down the gauntlet. It won't work
a second time.

As we walked round the banks we met Nick G., who
re-invited me to fish at his hotel's private carp pond.
Naturally, I said I'd see him there next month.

Time for a proper tea, with scrambled eggs on toast,
bread and bramble jelly, Clare's fruit loaf and the blackbirds singing through the open window. Then down to
Forked Pond where, along the track to the water, we
heard the 'chook-chook' of a nightingale. We had to stop
and listen more closely. There were two, either side of the
track in dense hawthorn bushes. That means I've heard
four this week – after not hearing any in England these
last ten years.

It was a pity we bumped into the bailiff, though he's a
nice enough fellow. It's just that his presence prevented
us from whooping like schoolboys at the sight of so

many big fish or making even wilder exclamations when I spotted a probable thirty-pound common carp up at the left-hand fork.

Much later, after Rollo had gone home and the sun had set, Clare and I walked over to Frensham Minor where the resinous pines and the mist-shrouded pond were mixing a sublime perfume. We heard a great fish roll on the surface, far out, and then a nightjar began to churr.

A nightjar and a nightingale on the same day! And to round it off perfectly, at midnight, lying in bed just before sleep, we heard a badger's chuckle.

These are good omens, I think.

Sunday 24th

Rod's speech at the opening meeting of the Carp Society was great fun and well-received. I followed with a far more explosive delivery. After discussing the modern carp angler's unhealthy obsession with statistics, science and technology, I demonstrated the dangers of modern carp baits – using a mixture of flour, casein and gunpowder! Were my unsuspecting audience choking because of the smoke or because they were laughing so much? I couldn't tell, but, afterwards, as Rod and I sat down together for a drink, people kept coming up to say how much they'd enjoyed the show. And I'd quite enjoyed the day, despite the distance I'd had to travel; it was good to see Rod again as well as meet a few other angling friends that I hadn't seen for a while, but as I drove home I couldn't help wondering about the value of such an event. I much prefer small, local gatherings to big conference-style jamborees. What, ultimately, are they *for*?

Good luck to the Carp Society. I'll probably see them again one day. But I much prefer the Golden Scale Club.

Saturday 30th

Noel came round to see us this afternoon, just as Clare was packing her bags. She's off to Crete next week with Jane, leaving me and the carp to get to know each other better throughout the whole of June. I might neglect to tidy the cottage, I might not make more than beans on toast for dinner, I might not sleep in my bed much, but I'm going to see lots of glorious sunrises and sunsets.

Leaving Clare to check she had everything she needed for her trip, Noel and I strolled over to the Wells to ogle at fish. The carp were looking languid, as if they knew they still had a fortnight before they have to start dodging us. As we watched them I realised where the G.S.C.

should open the new season. We had considered a pioneering expedition to the still largely unknown Pitchfords Pond, but the Wells was really a more suitable venue. Noel agreed. It means we can all meet at the cottage on the 15th and, after suitable refreshment, *walk* to the water at midnight.

JUNE

Monday 15th

The new season starts tomorrow and I would've liked to have spent the day sorting out my tackle which was still all jumbled in a bag after the end of last season. It would've been nice, also, just to have sat for a few hours alone on the banks of a quiet unsuspecting pond, dreaming of all the great fish that might happen for me. But, instead, I had to cycle to Hazlemere station to catch the 9.30am to Waterloo. Work shouldn't come first, I know, but if this last job turns out OK I'll have – hopefully – all the rest of the month for fishing. By 11.00am, I'd delivered my film to the processors and then cycled up Charing Cross Road to Anglebooks, where I spent a happy hour leafing through some lovely old fishing titles: *A Creel of Willow*, *At the Tail of the Weir*, *Days Among the Pike and Perch*. Bought W.G. Clifford's *Angling Jaunts and Jottings* and Howard Marshall's *Reflections on a River*. Bargain price, too! Then I went and sat in the sun on a bench in Covent Garden while I scribbled the opening of my next article for *Angling* magazine. Finally, at 1.00pm, I took a deep breath and went back to the processors, hoping desperately that the shots – of a spinning coin – had all worked. Laughed as I looked at them on the light box. They had! Rushed them round to Bedford Square where they were gratefully received by Heinemann; then onward to meet Rick for lunch and make final plans for our first casts, at midnight.

Just before 4.00pm I was rattling back at speed over Waterloo Bridge on the Hercules, which got me to the station only seconds before the Hazlemere train. So, though I had, after all, quite enjoyed my day in Crazy-land, it was still very blissful to be travelling away from it again – away to where trees gradually outnumbered buildings and where, just after the little station at Witley, the train rumbled past a rather nice reed-fringed lake.

The cottage was cool and welcoming when I came in. I unparcelled my two new old books and laid them on the table before making a pot of tea. Savoured a very pleasant hour before a rude knock on the door disturbed my reverie. It was Noel, aka Trottingshawe, Treasurer of the Golden Scale Club. Naturally he wasn't here to discuss non-payment of subs: all he wanted to do was wind some new line on to his reel, share another pot of tea with me and await the arrival of the rest of the rabble. First, though: we had to collect a barrel of Gales ale that I'd ordered from the Prince and, also, collect the Chairman, Nick (Dandy), who was due in at the station at 7.00pm. Algy was waiting in the garden when we got back, hiding in the bushes because he knew we'd be carrying blow-pipes. After we'd flushed him out with dough pellets, we all set off through the woods to inspect this season's Opening Night Venue: the Wells. The carp were gliding unconcernedly through the dark reflections, much to our delight. Algy became suddenly very nostalgic for those magical nights of our youth when we'd fish remote and often forbidden carp pools; and when the reflected stars were mysteriously wobbled by unseen things moving below the surface. I told him that, with the conditions so perfect, we'd be reliving that magic again soon.

By the time we'd walked back the one and a half miles through the trees, Rick (Birtwhistle) was rolling down the lane from the village. Good timing, as we were, by then, very hungry and thirsty. The barrel of beer was on the table under the apple tree and Rick had the food and a barbecuing engine in the boot of his car.

As the evening darkened and the first star appeared, I lit the torches and we raised our glasses to the new season. Everyone was impressed by the quality of the ale – and the supper was excellent. We made a few optimistic plans for the coming weeks, some of them almost realistic, some completely absurd (possible: a Victorian-style gudgeon party in punts on the Thames; impossible: an expedition up the Yorkshire Derwent – to find the last burbot in England). To the mild amusement of the rest of the company, I reflected on this day (still, just, the 15th) last year, when, on my way to Redmire Pool, I posted cards to Nick and Rick informing them that I was

about to break the twenty-eight-year-old carp record.
Algy said the whole story, including the carp, was just a
figment of my imagination. And as the kind of fishing we
do is really just like dreaming we had to agree that he was
probably right.

Typically, because we had to finish the barrel, because
we then had to make several pots of tea back in the
cottage, because we foolishly decided to tackle up *before*
netting out and because some people couldn't find their
rods and so had to borrow some of mine, it was well past
midnight by the time we were on our way.

Tuesday 16th

It was a real pleasure to be able to walk to a water
rather than drive, especially on the opening night and
when our path took us through such lovely moonlit
country. Though we were walking under tall beech trees
for most of the way we had a suddenly open sky above us
when we skirted the village cricket ground; and the pale
blue glow to the north-west showed us that dawn wasn't
far away.

By the time we were approaching the pool we had
walked off the effects of the alcohol. Also our senses were
made sharper by the various lovely scents of the woods,

scents that were finally all overcome by the sweet green-house air that always hangs over a still water on a summer night when everything is calm. Our steps became slower and softer and our voices became whispers as the path led us down to the reed bed at the pool's head.

The water looked black and glassy. There was no mist, despite the slight chill. We paused for a few minutes while deciding where around the pool we'd fish. Naturally we had the place to ourselves as night fishing was forbidden. Our presence, though, was perfectly acceptable as G.S.C. members have a divine right to fish whenever and wherever they pleased (Rule 6b). Nick said he'd like to fish between the lily beds, Algy chose a spot between the lilies and an overhanging tree. Trottingshawe, Rick and I preferred the look of the deeper more open water along the opposite bank. Within a few minutes we had all settled quietly into our chosen places and cast our baits.

As I was the only one familiar with the pool I'd recommended that we all use floating crust as it was the bait that nearly always worked best last season. However, because the air was cool, it might've been more productive if we'd fished something, like beans or corn on the bottom. It didn't matter though, in that first hour, what we used or how we fished; we were simply glad to be back in our favourite dimension.

Gradually the pale glow above the dark treetops

strengthened and the stars began to fade. Our crusts, floating motionless in the reedy margins, became more visible on the still dark-looking water; yet though the water was dark I suddenly became aware of a darker shape drifting slowly past, just beneath the surface. The carp were on the move and for several minutes I seemed to hold my breath as three more fish, one of them a clear twenty-pounder, ghosted by, close to my bait. My expectations rose as a carp turned towards me, but then the tension was broken by a great splash over on the far bank. A reel screeched and I looked up to see the shadowy form of an angler struggling to control a powerful adversary. It was Nick. 'Bring me a net!' he shouted. 'I think this is quite a good fish.' I got round to him just as the carp ploughed through the lily bed on his left, yet he managed to force it back into open water where, after a few loud echoing splashes, it rolled into the net.

The first carp of the new season: an eleven-pounder, and it made Nick a very happy angler, so happy that he decided not to cast again. He lay back, smiling, against a grassy tussock and fell asleep. The rest of us were convinced there'd be more chances, but the commotion caused by Nick's fish had obviously spooked the rest of the carp colony. We didn't even glimpse another fish for the rest of the morning. The dawn chorus rose and fell, the sun beamed down on us over the treetops, yet by 10.00am we all decided it was time to walk back home for breakfast. Also, Nick had to catch a train back to Crazyland and Algy had to fly a plane back to some foreign country. But Rick, Noel and I were eager to cast again and by 1.00 we were sitting in the cool parlour of the Black Horse, Nuthurst, enjoying a bit of lunch before driving the last mile to the delectable Sheepwash. After paying our respects at the farm we walked across the fields to the willow-shaded pool and found it looking – and feeling – as lovely as ever.

We went down to the shallows and I was pleased to see thick weed growth there, like there was the very first time we cast here. I fished the same little gap in the trees and bushes as I did when I hooked a ten-pounder, seven years ago. The third cast (with four grains of corn) was the best, dropping the bait right next to the weedbed over to my left – in front of the leaning oak.

I leant the faithful old rod – the Mk IV – on a twig and sat back in the grass. For a minute or two my sleep-lessness began to creep up on me and, like Nick at the Wells, I began to nod off. But then I was suddenly wide awake with my eye sharply focused on the line from the rod-tip. After a few moments, the angle of the line altered from diagonal to near-horizontal and I struck into a fish that charged along the edge of the weedbed. There was a pleasant solidity at the end of the line and the rod bent over. The carp surfaced, made a big splash, plunged, thrashed on the surface again, then dived for the oak branches on my left. I put on maximum pressure and managed to turn it. It made a dive for the weeds but again side strain and severe pressure kept it in open water. Then it dived towards me and I had to wind like mad to keep in contact (I was using the new centre-pin). It rolled, then dived headlong into the weedbed over on my right and nothing I could do would stop it.

For a while all was solid. I began to wonder whether I would have to go in. Rick and Trottingshawe were standing next to me – Rick with the net – and they both voiced their encouragements as I raised the rod high, provoking the fish to lash out with its tail. 'He doesn't like that!' said Rick. Gradually he worked himself towards the edge of the weeds. I finally eased it clear of them and enjoyed again that great relief that comes when a snagged fish is running in the open once more. There were a few more dives and turns in the narrow strip of clear water. Then I got him over the net and Rick lifted him up. A typical Sheepwash carp – long, lean, but very solid and dark-toned. This was an all-scaled mirror, with a splendidly large tail. Weight, 6lbs+.

I had one more bite and that was from a 1½lbs tench. Rick gave up carp-fishing and began catching roach instead. Trottingshawe did not give up carp-fishing and caught nothing. We had to pack at teatime so that Rick could drive us home and then go off trout fishing. Trout fishing! On the 16th! The man's a lunatic! But then he is President.

34

Trottingshawe and I had a leisurely tea back at the cottage. Then at 9.00pm we got our tackle and once more trod the tree-hung path to Waggoners. The sun was going down over the cricket pitch and the cricketers were practising.

By the time we got to the pool it was almost a year to the minute that I'd hooked my fifty-one-pounder – though I didn't even think of it at the time. And the pool was nearly empty of anglers! The last three were just packing up and by 10.00pm there were only us two, and the bats and the carp and the silence and the moon rising. But the carp had obviously not yet recovered from the shock of the sudden invasion of fishermen. They were not yet inclined to do much feeding, even though one or two crusts did go down. We fished till 11.30pm, then wound in and left the pool in perfect peace. We walked back through the dark woods and as I came in through the cottage door the clock was striking midnight.

Thursday 18th

The 17th had been cold and grey and I hadn't had any urge to fish. But today I had to write *two* articles for *Angling* and where better to write them than the banks of a carp lake? I went to Shillinglee and was delighted to discover only one other angler on the vast water. I went and fished from the platform in the reed beds, casting a hook full of chickpeas to the edge of the lilies.

It was hot in the sun, as I sat and scribbled away at my new piece – 'Historic Blanks'! After a couple of hours the sun had gone behind dark clouds and I guessed I might have a chance of finding a feeding fish. So, having finished the first article, I set off to wade through the reeds and eventually found a bubbling carp, by a willow island and between two big lily beds. I cast next to the left-hand bed and waited for nearly two hours as the fish moved through the pads and bubbled in open water. Maybe I need to educate them into taking chicks. I wished I'd brought some crust and a tin of corn. Still, next time I'll come altogether better prepared. The place I fished has seemingly never been fished before and it's a perfect holding spot for the elusive Shillinglee carp. Next time I'll bring some wood and make a hidden platform. Perhaps a bit of float-fished corn will do the trick with the monsters.

I went back to the reed-bed platform and quickly wrote my second article. Time was getting on and I had to catch the post. I packed up at 5.25pm and just made Hazlemere in time. (Luckily there was a stamp machine!)

After tea, I decided to return to the Wells, though I didn't leave until 9.20pm, walking again through the evening woods. I wasn't expecting such a pleasant surprise on arriving at the pool. There wasn't a soul there! But though I fished quietly and steadily, I never even had a sniff from a carp. Only about three free crusts were clooped at, and I didn't see any actually disappear.

As the sky cleared of high cloud and the moon shone on the treetops, I reeled in and walked home through the dark. No owls called, no fox barked; the woods were completely silent.

Sunday 21st – (Solstice) Redmire

Arrived at about 7.00pm, on a bright and very warm evening. Roy had been at the pool since midday, his eager enthusiasm obvious from his whispered speech and his staring eyes. (It was his first session at Redmire since 1977.) He was set up in the Ash Grove, a place I'd mentally chosen on my way to Redmire, seeing that the wind was easterly. But then Roy mentioned the fact that the only fish caught the previous week were taken from the shallows. The hot weather was keeping the carp in the weedbeds off the islands and they'd been moving into the shallows in the evening. So, as the sun began to slope to the edge of the grassy hill opposite, I began to creep up to the head of the pool. I fished from the willow-bole, casting with corn-baited hook and bated breath. Ripples glided up to me and past me. A dark shadow approached, hesitated, then cruised away. The line never moved. I moved quietly to Wasp Island, casting two rods into the slowly rocking and heaving water. The carp were there in numbers, but they weren't interested in corn. I should have gone and got some fresh bait – salmon eggs or broad beans – but I didn't. I sat patiently into fading light, watching the slowly shifting water and listening to the odd big fish roll or leap. I had a slow take, which I missed, badly. By 11.30 there was still a clear glow in the north-west. The water gradually became flat and calm and I guessed that the carp were moving back into the deeps. So I went over to the Ash Tree, put out a bait beneath the branches (with the pipe) and settled down for the night.

Monday 22nd

The night was cold, but I woke as a warming sun rose and heard the cry of a curlew. Was I dreaming? I'd never heard a curlew at Redmire before. As the dawn turned into morning and the sun grew hot, I got up and had breakfast under the oaks, with Roy. John Supergillie arrived as we ate and after greeting him and making him a cup of tea I told him I was going to try and catch a fish from the top of the island tree. I sat up there, in the blazing sun, for two hours, dropping crusts beyond basking carp, then drawing them gently back over the fishes' noses. I had not even a sniff of appreciation. I did, however, behold the marvellous sight of *two* curlews circling in a powerful thermal. They whirled higher and higher into the blue until I lost them in the glare of the sun. I've never seen curlews circling like that before.

After the great heat of the day, I expected to do great things in the evening. The sky began to look thundery and oppressive. Black clouds, red-rimmed, began to rise up. But the pool was mysteriously quiet and lifeless. Nothing moved, and after three hours of tense expectations, my suspicions were confirmed. There was a great thrashing of water in the weedbeds. The Redmire carp had begun to spawn.

Tuesday 23rd/Wednesday 24th

The frenzied ritual went on all the next day and it was quite a spectacle as the fish charged and surged through the weeds. For hour after hour the big males chased the even bigger females, making a sound like a herd of cattle stampeding through the shallows. By evening of the 23rd, they began to quieten. I had a take from the island

on float tackle, but missed. I fished the shallows, again
expecting great things after the expending of energy, but,
fishing with beans, I had not a bite. Not a bite at dawn on
the 24th, though I predicted a fish on the coming night.
Set up on the island as darkness fell.

Thursday 25th

Woke from a deep dream to the sound of a constantly
screaming centre-pin reel. For a second I hesitated, then
I leaned forward and grabbed the 'B. B.' that was rattling
on the plank, its reel spinning fast. As soon as I'd picked
it up, I felt a long, fast, heavy pull that dragged the rod-
point down. I kept the pressure steady, with the rod held
low to keep the line clear of the trailing branches. The
reel stopped singing and I began to haul. There was a
fierce lunge and the reel sang again.

In the half-light, I'd seen a vague commotion out in
the weedbed and the splash had sounded hefty. I thought
I'd hooked a big one. It sulked in the middle of the
weeds, but gentle, even pressure soon had it coming back
and once I'd got it moving, it came through the aqua-
growth fairly easily. I felt the slow throb-throb of the tail
working and was ready when the fish made another dive
away.

Over in the east an orange half-moon was breaking through the cloud and, in the north-east, the new dawn was glowing. In its light I strained to see any signs of carp, as I brought it up to the island. I was kneeling on the plank bridge, the rod low and the fish coming in very close to an alder branch. The line must have missed it by inches. It thrashed in the clear margins and I knew then it wasn't as big as I'd hoped. But it dived away again, heading over to my right, and got well stuck in the weeds. I put the pressure on from higher up and after an anxious few seconds, out he came. I held on tight after that and in a few more moments the net was under him and I lifted gently. Ah well: he was, at least, a very good-looking fish; a high-backed and darkly golden double-figured common carp, and a fine christening for the Bernithan Beauty.

The skylarks were warbling as I gently lowered him back into the pool. Then, after recasting, I dropped myself back to sleep, lying not very comfortably, half on the platform and half on the island.

Nothing was moving later in the morn, though I put a bait out in the weedbeds where I knew the carp were skulking. As the day got brighter, with even a gleam of sunshine, one or two carp moved on to the shallows. I fished for them from Wasp Island, but though I saw them go down over my blowpiped corn, they wouldn't look at a hook bait.

Went into Ross at teatime, to pick up my van that was being 'dealt with' (MOTs are so boring, but I try to be partly legal). John and I had a pint in the pub garden, below Ross bridge, and watched a young fisherman land a grilse from the parapet. Back at the pool, all was subdued for a few hours. I looked out over the shallows and saw not a fish. But I had a feeling there would be one feeding along the edge of the weeds and, sure enough, just between Keffords and the Stile, there was a big patch of rising bubbles. First it was on the edge of the weeds, then between the weedbed and the bank and a careful cast dropped the corn a little too accurately – smack in the middle of the bubble-cloud. But they carried on for a few moments – then stopped. The line began to angle away towards the weeds and as it tightened, I struck hard; the hook flew past me into the branches of an alder!

I put two rods out from the island – one to the left and one way out in the middle of the weeds. Then, after making myself a lot more comfortable than last night, I dozed off and woke to hear the call of the curlew at about 5.00am. Nothing had come to the baits and I dozed off again for a couple of hours, then got up to a cold, grey, blustery morning and went to make breakfast in the hut. Tippett was playing on the radio as I had my boiled eggs and tea.

I walked up the grassy slope afterwards, just to enjoy

the view of the distant hills and have a different perspective on the pool. A few minutes after I got back to the island, the indicator on the right-hand rod jammed against the butt-ring as the line streamed out. I raised the rod and felt something dive deep into the weeds. However, I soon drew him free as he was only a small one. I was glad to see him though: a five-pound fully-scaled mirror. I was especially pleased as he'd picked up a *blowpiped* bait.

I settled down to write a couple of letters, one to R. Walker, who is worryingly ill, and one to Nick. As I was finishing the first sentence of Nick's, I heard the flick of foil over the plank-bridge and before the line had time to tighten I struck on the 'B.B.' and was into the second carp of the morning. It just plunged about under the branches for a while and the rod top took the strain well. I tightened up the drag on the centre-pin and then the fish made a short run into the weeds. I soon got him back. He made a run over to the right and I saw he wasn't a monster. He slogged around, back and forth, and churned about a lot when I got the net in the water. But there were no dangerously long runs and I eventually eased him over the mesh. A portly hump-backed, small-tailed and small-headed common carp of exactly 12 lbs. I took his portrait, which should make a nice print, and then it was time to go home.

The curlew called, long and hauntingly, as he went down over the far side of the valley. The wind blew strongly and very cold. Midsummer seemed a long time ago.

Tuesday 30th – The Wells

Arrived to find four too many anglers. But the carp were hanging about in the shallows and I cast a 'seanip' next to a sunken branch. One or two fish went right under it – it'd have been interesting to have hooked one – on 3lb line!

Went back in the evening and found the place wonderfully deserted. In the half-light, I saw a dark shape hanging in the reflection of the oak. I sat under the tree until there was only a glimmer of blue in the west. One or two fish had taken the free offerings and I knew I'd come close to having the bait taken also. But at 11.00pm I reeled in and left the pool to the bats, owls and eager midges.

JULY

Thursday 2nd – Star Pool

An auspicious occasion, it being the first fishing of Rollo and myself. The first casting of lines together and across and generally into tangles and knots. I arrived an hour late at our rendezvous – the Star, at Heathfield – and I think he was just about to give up on me. But after a few 'Look here Yates!'s and 'Where the bloody hell have you been?!'s he calmed down sufficiently to be able to enjoy a quiet pint in the empty bar of the pub. We hadn't really decided where to fish, as we had quite a choice of waters in the vicinity. But, after a short and fierce debate, it had to be the Star Pool; the traditional old-carp-anglers' water. We paid our money to the farmer's wife and made our way through the farmyard, where the cows were calmly lowing, waiting to be milked.

Down by the pool, there was silence. Not a soul, thank goodness, and not a ripple of even a breeze on the water – just a few rudd-rings opening out by the weedbeds. I say weedbeds, yet the weeds were almost non-existent. Apparently the farmer had been advised to remove them to lessen pressure on the dam! Carp were jostling the reed stems and for the first hour we tried for them. Foolishly I waded out with a rod, leaving another on the bank to fish for itself. Naturally, I had a bite then on the abandoned rod (tut, tut).

At around sunset, I sneaked along the bank and discovered a good carp feeding close in. He was bubbling and clouding and I got a hookfull of corn within inches of him without him noticing me. But he moved in the wrong direction. He began to feed under a leaning oak-branch and I could see he was a really good fish, a wildie of possibly 8 or 9lbs. I put the bait next to him and for a second I felt the fever of expectation, positive he was going to be hooked. But then, just down the bank, Lawrence missed a carp and began to swear and curse. The fish in front of me seemed to notice the commotion and cruised lazily away. I went over to see Lawrence, wielding a large stick in my hands. Eventually, though, that same carp returned to the leaning bough and he went right over the bait, but refused it.

The sun had set and we decided to have a last hour by the sunken willow on the opposite side of the pond. Lawrence led the way round and he fished on the right of the tree while I dropped two baits in the margins to the left. The light lingered in the west but the pool began to darken. I saw the first star. Lawrence crept along the overgrown path to see how I was doing. We talked in whispers about the carp, about rods and bait. I was just going to describe a deadly new idea for a carp bait, when the scrap of silver foil on the left-hand rod slid over to the butt-ring. I reached down and struck, gently. For a second I wasn't sure that I'd hooked a carp at all. It just hung near the surface, not doing anything. Then it began to plunge and I felt the line ping against an unseen branch. As I cleared it, the fish splashed and turned to our left, making a long run parallel to the bank. The old Aerial screeched and I leant out with the rod, trying to keep the line clear of the bankside trees. Lawrence ran off for his net. The line was only 3lb b.s. I must have been mad to have thought that any carp I hooked next to the old willow would be held on such light tackle. Sure, I was mad. But then so was that carp; he'd run the wrong direction – *away* from the willow!

I slowed and stopped him and the rod-top throbbed and then began to relax. But just as I began to ease him back, there was a surge of power, a splash and the reel began to sing once more. The splash seemed to be miles away. For a while it was a to and fro pulling match; then he began to come quite easily and the ratchet clicked as I wound the line back. Lawrence peered round the leaning branches as he stood in the margins with the net. In the half-light a silver bow wave was clearly visible, leading straight towards him.

The angle of pull began to change as the carp swung out from the bank. Then all went solid. He'd got me round a clump of weeds. I eased the pressure, then tightened up and reached over with the rod. But there was no dislodging it. I felt life, though, stirring on the end of the line. I slacked right off and we could see the line lying loose on the surface. It began to slide away and I followed its tightening with the rod-top until the very last moment – then lifted. It was free. Ah, bliss! To have a carp well and truly stuck and then to feel that unhindered movement again is like suddenly triumphing over a devilish crossword puzzle. But it was still a tricky struggle, at close quarters, and the fish could've had the last word. It circled dangerously near the willow branches and seemed to appear on the surface first to the left and then, magically, ten feet to the right before I knew what was happening. The old Walker Avon bent nicely and I brought him nearer to the net. He was off again in a flash, but then, next time, I kept his head well up and Lawrence lifted smoothly. There was a whoop of victory from both of us as the carp was safely enmeshed. We laid him in the grassy field behind us. A beautiful, clean looking wildie. Just over 4lbs.

A good moment to pack up. As we strolled round the pool the last of the day was hanging behind the trees, which were reflected blackly in the pond. It was absolutely silent, except for the sound of water gushing over the sluice.

After a superior Chinese supper (I'll have to remember that restaurant) we went for a couple of midnight hours at one of the Isfield AS lakes. I liked it, from what I could see of it, and Lawrence said he'd seen some mighty carp there. The last one he'd hooked had smashed his oldest (and dearest) rod. We set up near a reedy island and after a few minutes I had a creepy sort of run on sweetcorn and hooked a spirited 2lb tench. I had two more, both on corn. Then a few crusts began to go down and I ended up sitting on a landing-stage by a reed bed, trying to tempt two fish at once. The larger of the pair had slurped down a crust in good old-fashioned style, just to the right of the reeds, while the smaller one had sipped down a crust from the very edge of the bed on the left. Of course every time I tried for one, the other made his presence felt and so I recast for him. The worst example of my chopping and changing came when I'd pulled the hook out of a bit of drifting crust, so I could put on a fresh piece and drop it onto the clooping fish out in the reeds. As I rebaited, *schloop!* – down went the drifting bait – to the big one. It was an enjoyable couple of hours, though: the night was warm and there were even three short, soft showers of rain. As I drove home, the dawn light was rising in the north-east.

Sunday 5th

Went down for a bit of work on Pitchfords Pond. God! It looked like a bowling green. Just a sheet of duck-weed from bank to bank and only a tiny square of open water in the centre of the main pool. There were four of us engaged in the hearty hauling of weedbeds and reeds and the clearing of the feeder stream: Rick, alias Birtwhistle, Noel, alias Trottingshawe, and Lawrence, alias Rollo. We put a drag through the feeder-pipe from the main stream and straight away we had more volume of water coming in. The level began to rise and we hoped that it would go over the dam and take the duck-weed with it.

Most memorable moments of the afternoon were, one, when Rick was walking down the meandering feeder-stream in chest waders, where it was eighteen inches wide and nearly three feet deep. And, two, when he, Lawrence and I crossed out on to the island by the fallen tree. A really *exciting* place to fish from, giving good vantage points and having fallen willow boughs on one, very carpy-looking side.

We repaired to The Anglers Rest at Barcombe Mills for refreshment and after that, just as I was going to follow the example of Rick and Noel and go home, Lawrence persuaded me to have five minutes fishing a little moat he'd just discovered *in* Lewes. We had a look round; not terribly picturesque, but the water was clear and there were nice looking weedbeds. As we strolled along the banks a carp slurped down a big bit of crust and we ran back to the vehicles for our gear. We'd soon cast out. But then Lawrence spotted fish rising from the end of the moat, where crusts had drifted up to the over-flow. He beckoned me over there after a minute and I crept next to him and flicked out a little bit of bread. A carp made an exuberant attack on the free crust and my heart thumped as it attacked the bait. It disappeared! I waited until I was sure the line was moving, then struck. A common crashed through the surface and I moved right to steer it away from the feeding area. I got it to about fifteen yards along the bank, then the hook went. We both cursed. But the fish were still taking crust and in a few minutes my bait again went under – quite fiercely (none of your tentative, shy lipping – just a straight and splashy WOMP!). This was a bigger fish. He worked the surface, like the other one. Then dived and it was a while before I could get him clear of the swim. I played him out next to a biggish weedbed and he fought incredibly hard. The Avon (No. III) was in a tight half-circle and though I knew it wasn't any monster, the clutch on the Ambidex, with 8lb line, kept rasping and buzzing. Lawrence came up with the net. Six pounds and a bit. I was surprised, I thought it had to be twice that weight, at least.

The carp were still feeding. Lawrence missed a couple of chances. I got another fish, out of the weeds this time, though only a young common. We packed up at 11.00pm. I think I'll be back there, soon.

Monday 6th

After an afternoon in London (did find a(nother) nice fishing book) it was pleasant indeed to sit by the Wells for a couple of hours after sunset, with the carp moving cautiously for the baits and just rocking the water here and there. They certainly aren't easy to tempt here, not when you consider the sort of fishing I was enjoying last night.

Thursday 7th – The Golden Scale Club Throws a Gudgeon Party

A perfect summer morning to drive down to Cookham with Clare (aka Gaffer) and Noel (aka Trottingshawe) for this year's G.S.C. gudgeon party. At a small and nicely shabby boatyard we met only three other members, Dandy, Birtwhistle and Gnasher. There had been enthusiastic talk earlier of a full turnout and a fleet of punts heading up the Thames, emulating the grand Victorian tradition of massed gudgeon fishing. However, everyone had come dressed for the part, with straw boaters, blazers and cricket whites, while the female contingent sported lovely vintage finery that they'd obviously nicked from their great-grandmothers' wardrobes. It would've been better, though, if Jasper had come as he would, as always, have made a refreshing contrast in his motorbike leathers and cowboy boots. So, instead of a flotilla, we hired a single punt and, because Trott didn't like the concept of the punting pole, a rowing boat.

Having tackled up on the bank, we headed gently downstream towards an avenue of big willow trees where we moored and began to fish. No one in the party had actually caught a Thames gudgeon for years; in fact the only one of us who'd even fished the river in the last decade was Birty. But we were confident; after all, when we were schoolboys we used to be able to fill a keep-net with Thames gudgeon in an afternoon – and that was when our tackle was even more knotted and rudimentary than it is now. Today, we used ridiculously light gear and wincingly tiny hooks; we baited with a single maggot and trotted little crow quill floats alongside the trailing branches, but for an hour no one had anything other than pretend bites – 'Look! That was a bite!' No it wasn't; the hook just snagged the riverbed – but it made everyone look.

Writing in *At the Tail of the Weir*, Patrick Chalmers said: 'Twenty dozen gudgeon to a punt was no uncommon basket.' But he was describing a day's gudgeon fishing in the nineteenth century, when the Thames above London was still a lush clear stream, when the local riverside hostelries would cook your gudgeon like whitebait and sell you a bottle of champagne to wash them down for seven shillings. Yet there were, apparently, still plenty of fish in the river and we couldn't quite understand how we'd failed to catch any of them.

Just upstream of us was a wooded island that made a perfect setting for lunch. The picnic was tasty and ample, the sun warm and the river looked more promising by

the time we were afloat again. We tried a new, slightly deeper stretch along the southern bank and at least we started catching fish, but they were chub. They weren't very big, but a pound chub can *feel* big when you hook it on delicate tackle and a light rod, and we pretended we were hauling in monstrous gudgeon. Eventually, Trottingshawe, fishing in his rowing boat, claimed to have caught a genuine gudgeon, but as he flipped it back in the water we were sure it looked more like a minnow.

The sun began to sink into the upstream willows and it was time to punt back to the boatyard. We thanked old George, the boatman, who had been pleased with the look of our wooden rods and period dress, and was glad we'd enjoyed our day. We ended up in his recommended Cookham pub and had a wondrous evening talking about rivers, ponds, boats and all the gudgeon we'd nearly caught.

Sunday 12th – Redmire

There was a thrush singing beautifully as I stopped the van after rolling down the grassy slope to the trees by the water's edge. It was wonderful to be back and have the lovely place all to myself. Walked right around the pool with a rod as soon as I'd got there, at about 3.00pm, but there was nothing moving anywhere. I put a quill and a bunch of maggots out under the oaks and after a minute I had a good bite, which I missed. I knew why. It was a nice little gudgeon. Remembering our humiliating defeat by gobio last week, I put on a No.16, baited with three maggots, and cast again. Dip-dip went the quill and in came a wriggling, grey, blue-speckled wonder. I could still catch gudgeon! Next cast I hooked a real monster. A great, fat, bristling specimen that must have weighed nearly 2oz! Pity that I had a rather 'heavy'-looking bite a few minutes later and missed it, only to then see a big cloud of bubbles rising from the deeps.

After tea, I put a few bits on the island for the night, then got net and rods and followed the carp up to the shallows (this, after a quick look over the ridge into the west, where a white crack had appeared in the bars of cloud, just above the Black Mountains). There were quite a few fish moving ponderously around, close in. I put out (almond) corn-baited float tackle to the left and a bunch of maggots to the right. A fish came over the corn and bolted immediately! Not good, I thought, but fifteen minutes later another humping ripple began to disturb the water by the float and after a few seconds the float sank and the line drew gently taut. For some reason I was surprised when I connected. There was a big splash and the fish bolted away and to the left. The reel buzzed and the wave went out and then harder to the left. The old Avon went into its familiar, alarming curve, I got the fish out from the left-hand bank and he charged away, the line catching on a nasty sunken branch but luckily coming away with a sudden twang; out he went, then to the right, pushing into the thick weed that now covers most of the shallows. Seemed to stick but I knew I could get him moving and sure enough in he came plunging and turning into the unwieldy net. (The evening was grey and very warm.) An immaculate 'linear mirror' of 9lbs.

The carp were still moving despite the disturbances. Some were very big and I was tempted to move around to Wasp Island. I did, and put out two rods and never had a touch. The fish seemed to know I was there. It was dark as I went back down the overgrown bank.

Monday 13th

Woke feeling too hot and had to remove my pullover. Lay on my back in my sleeping bag, looking up at the grey sky between the leaves of the island willow. It was nearly dawn. A cock crowed, the distance of it making the sound curiously hollow. Then a swallow began to twitter and two skylarks went up, warbling softly. It was not quite 4.00am and I went back to sleep. For some reason, perhaps the previous short nights, I was exhausted and slept till 10.30am. Of course I woke up feeling as if I'd got an awful hangover. But a good wash and breakfast, followed by a stroll, soon brought me round to my senses.

Hardly a fish moving on the pool, the skies overcast and a slight breeze blowing. It's too warm though. I feel that a slight drop in temperature and a heavy fall of rain would do the fishing a world of good. Still, at least I know they'll be on the shallows this evening. At least I think I know that. Where shall I fish? The west or the east bank? Or Wasp Island? We shall see. I laugh, just thinking about it.

I'm sitting here on the island, leaning back against the stump with *three* rods out. Two in the margins and one in the middle of the weedbed. I don't think I'm in with much of a chance at the moment, so I think I'll go and have some tea and bread and cheese.

Took the punt out after my meal and cruised gently into the weedbeds where lay, basking, the carp. The fish didn't seem to mind me and I was able to drift right next to a mirror of upper thirties and a very big common. Suddenly the potential of my position was realised and I gently made for shore. Once there, I hurriedly got rod, net and a tin of maggots and, after baiting up, drifted back into the weedbeds.

The sun was hot on my back and my heart began to reverberate as I dapped for that same big mirror-carp with a bunch of maggots. But the punt drifted just too close and the fish became wary and cruised off. Didn't go far, though, and it came to rest next to a large common, just to my left. I paddled as quietly as I could and then dropped the bait on to the mirror's nose from about fifteen feet. It just hung there in the weeds and the bait was clearly visible right next to its face. The boat began to drift away in a gentle breeze and I had to use the paddle with one hand and hold the rod with the other. It seemed to understand what was going on – the fish, not the boat – and once more it swam quietly away, though the common remained and I dapped for him, but with no result. Eventually the breeze came up again and I couldn't hold my position. The carp sank from sight as I put the paddle in the water.

I went on up the lake and found a couple of fish who bolted as I approached, making huge swirls which opened great holes in the weeds. From above, it looked like a typhoon in a forest, as the long fronds of hornwort swayed round and round in the turbulence. I found a big, dark-looking carp and dropped the maggots next to him. He was lying with his tail towards me, and straight away he began to reverse and turn towards the bait, obviously interested. But then that devilish breeze sprang up and began to push me straight at the fish. It sank, but then seemed to decide that he wanted the maggots anyway and came back up for them. Too late! The punt was suddenly over him and I couldn't keep the bait in the same place. That was my last chance, the breeze remained steady and it was hopeless trying any further. I paddled for the Willow Pitch, floating over the crystal-clear depths with the long weed-cables reaching up to the surface.

It being a warm evening, it seemed a good idea to have a glass of ale up at Llangrove. 'How's Jack?' I asked the landlord as he poured me a glass of the excellent bitter (much improved since last time).

'He's there behind you!'

So it turned out to be two or three glasses of ale, as old Jack rambled on about his various adventures, some happy, some sad. He's been getting a few good trout from the Garren – 'Always carry a bit of tackle in my pocket – but never use a rod. You're buggered if you've got a rod.' He's got a good dog who sits with him while he fishes and cocks an ear for the slightest sound. 'I'm not fishing, just taking my dog for a walk!'

'Remember old Bunting? Dave,' he said, turning to Dave Bufton, 'he used to go and move the dead carp as rolled up after the spawning at Bernithan. He was in the punt one day and a fish came up with its head one side of the punt and the tail the other. That must have been a biggun!'

'You goin' to wroit a book?' he asked.

He told me of a sad sight up on the road. A mother partridge had been run over by a 'bloody stupid tanker driver' and the chicks were standing around her. Jack went up to the dead hen and found a young one nesting under its mother's wing. 'Why couldn't he have stopped and let them pass?' he said. Dave told me of a badger he'd like to see move back up to the ancestral sett below the bottom pond and also of a giant stoat he once tried to catch, but didn't. Jack told me a tale of a fishing expedition where he took one of the local lads on to the river and caught seven and the lad caught none.

'He wouldn't keep still, kept coming up the bank to see how I was doin'.'

He slipped the trout he'd caught into the lining of his jacket, but one slipped out on the way home. The lad went back and found it.

'Always cover your tracks! If you even make a footprint in a sandbar, wipe it out with a bit of stick. Never knock down the nettles.'

We could've chatted all evening. But it was 9.00pm and nearly sunset. I remembered my premonition that July 13th would be the day and so I said farewell to the jolly company and drove down into the sinking sun. Up in the shallows, hardly a fish stirred. I crept up with a rod but only saw one ripple. I cast next to the willows, on the opposite bank (after sneaking around) but everywhere seemed strangely silent. The pool was laughing at me for making my bold statement earlier. Never take Redmire for granted. I reeled in and a wave opened up where the bait had been. Never take the futility of your statements for granted, either.

The moon was white in the clear sky and a mist began to form on the pool. Two swans sailed by, pale against the black reflections. I boiled a kettle for tea and, as it was brewing, the sight of the swans and the thought of my earlier punt across the pool persuaded me to go for a nocturnal voyage. I took my steaming tea, carefully stepped into the punt and put my mug down on the seat; then, with the paddle, I pushed away from the bank and let the punt drift until it floated, becalmed, almost in the centre of the pool.

Where better to sip a late-night mug of tea than in a punt at Redmire under the moon? I just wished I'd remembered to bring some biscuits.

There was complete silence. No owls, no splashes on the surface, no traffic on the miles-distant Monmouth road. When I'd finished my tea I lay down on the boards, staring up at the stars (the moon was low to the south). The punt lay motionless on the water, yet I was conscious of a kind of vibration, as if I could feel the hidden stirrings of all those huge fish deep down below me.

A stray night breeze wandered through the oak trees on the east bank and soon passed by, but a trailing finger of a draught reached out and very gradually pushed the punt up the pool until it was floating more or less over Pitchford's Pit, the deepest point in Redmire.

I was slightly perturbed by the sudden memory of a story that BB had written somewhere, about a similar night voyage across the pool. He'd heard a strange bubbling after a while and realised that the punt had started to leak. There was no paddle, the craft was sinking, but by paddling wildly with his hands he just managed to get ashore before it was too late. (Swimming in deep weedy water at night is not recommended.) I felt the boards and they were reassuringly dry, but I was still slightly spooked. And then I heard a tremendous crash as a big carp leapt up and fell back. It wasn't right next to me, but it sounded like a breaching whale, and the outspreading ripple, though taking a strangely long time to reach me, rocked the punt slowly from side to side, making the stars wobble.

It may have all looked beautiful, but, after the walloping fish, there was also something almost eerie going on. I sat up. 'Steady as she goes,' I said, as I paddled slightly nervously back to shore.

Tuesday 14th

Slept late into the morning, then set out once more in the punt and came close to a couple of big fish with my dapped bunch of maggots. On the way back, just as I was drifting in front of Ingham's, I spotted a tremendous black shape, right on the bottom in about five feet of water. As I came up to it I could see it was an enormous common. Its great length stretched away through the weed-stems and I couldn't make out its total size until I was right over it. In the crystal clear water, I could then see every scale along its back. Without doubt, the second-biggest common carp I've seen, and the clearest view I've ever had of any of the Redmire monsters – certainly the *closest* I've been to one. I suppose it could have been one of the two monster commons that followed, like pages, the King of Redmire, Leviathan, when I saw him in July '79. How big, this one by Ingham's? Around 60lbs, and certainly not less than 55lbs.

As the drift took the punt directly above him, he (or she) made a sudden thrust forward, disappearing into the dense weeds and making the stems sway and swirl for a whole minute after it had gone.

To round off this memorable day, I saw a peregrine falcon, flying below the dam, being pursued by a swallow.

Had a couple of pints with Jack again and got back to the shallows at 8.30, well before sunset. Yet I might as well have stayed at the Arms – there wasn't a carp in sight. However, a fish rolled off the stumps and so I spent the evening there, with two baits out in the deeps and an article to write while I was waiting for a fish.

Fish began to roll regularly after dark. The moon rose, bright and clear, and in its light I could see the occasional upburst of white spray and, once, a great carp, turning out in the weeds, only a few yards from me. Only had one twitch all night, and I bet that was from an eel.

Wednesday 15th

Crept round the pool at dawn and found not a fish to cast to.

In all, a very quiet few days, the same as all the previous mid to late July trips of previous years. Obviously a time to watch for a sudden change in conditions, and if there's no change and everything remains warm and calm, then it's a time to be patient.

Sunday 19th – River Rye (North Yorks)

An enjoyable day on the river, fishing with two spellbound prizewinners of a wildlife/fishing quiz and blowpipe competition. It was a great relief to see both of them catch plenty of fish (the youngest had never caught a fish before) and John, the eldest, landed two very good dace. I was encouraged to go back in the evening, after they'd gone triumphantly home, and try for a big dace myself. But it was too late and I couldn't see the quill, so I tied on a bigger hook and free-lined for chub with cheese. I fished from a high bank below shallows, letting the bait drift under an overhanging bush. After half an hour the line went strangely slack and I connected with a fish that had moved out into mid-river. On 3lb line I had quite a tussle on my hands: the reel screeched and the rod throbbed as I worked what I hoped was a big chub out of the weedbeds and up to the surface. After a few minutes I had him under the rod-point. Then, in the half-light, I saw a long pale shape turn on the dark water. A bloody great eel! I lost it.

Wednesday 22nd – The Wells

After a day of rain I thought I'd be in with a good chance for the carp and sneaked over to the lily beds at 8.30pm. Nothing moved all evening.

Thursday 23rd – Pitchfords

Again it was raining and the evening was cool. The two stalwarts Lawrence and Trott were already there when I arrived, but they hadn't caught anything. It was nothing serious, our fishing; we just wanted a rudd or tench from the weeds. But only Lawrence had a bite and after an hour, with the rain steadily increasing after a welcome, sweet-scented lull, we adjourned to the nearby pub for a couple of pints and a bite to eat. Trott produced the pictures of my first Redmire carp of the season and they inspired us out into the wet night, to have a go at the 'easy' fish of the moat. But, once again, only Lawrence had a bite, and he missed it.

Saturday 25th – Sheepwash

Met John by the farm at 8.45am and he was full of enthusiasm for the mild summer morning, the prospects of a carp and the very fact that he was going fishing. As we tackled up, a carp began to suck at the weeds only a few yards from us and with encouragement from me, John soon cast out a few grains of corn into the floating weed stems, not far from the slurping lips. But the fish moved up the pool, feeding as he was going. We moved to the next pitch and, with a blowpipe, put the bait only a few feet from him. For a while, the carp disappeared and I said we must hope for him to reappear right next to the bait, which he did. He took it, too, after only a few seconds' hesitation. But a gust of wind blew up and we couldn't see whether the line was tightening. I should've given the word to strike – we shouldn't have hesitated once those lips had gone down with the bait. As it was, we just waited, John tense with anticipation, for a sign that he'd taken properly. Eventually, he struck, just for the hell of it. Hopeless, of course.

I nearly had a chance myself, down in the shallows, but again the wind ruined my chances. Ended up fishing from a tree, casting right over the feeding carp who were 'tenting' in the weeds. John sneaked off into the prohibited area and actually hooked a good fish, which got off.

At lunchtime, we went to meet Lawrence in the Black

Horse and after a few pints and a beef roll we went back to try for the carp again. John left at 4.00pm, Lawrence at 7.00pm. I waited until sunset and had two carp right under my bait, over in the little lily bed in the corner. But I never had a chance for either of them.

Tuesday 28th

On a warm, sultry evening, I drove down the old southern route to Sheepwash, meeting Trott in the Black Horse, and getting to the pool at sunset. We dumped our stuff in our chosen pitches: Trott opposite the mid-willow, me in the Sticks. Then we went and found some fish surface-feeding in the shallows. But they didn't stay there long.

As the light faded I stalked surface feeders with corn, over in the restricted zone. What a pity I didn't have any crust. I came very close, but the carp couldn't suck the little grains through the dense mesh of weed-stems. A crust would've been fine. When it was too dark to see, I crept back to the Sticks and cast out a bait to either side. Then I made a cup of tea and called Trott over to join me.

The night was cool and a mist began to form. I lay in my bag on the hard clay bank, not sleeping very well. At about 2.30pm I had a run on the left-hand rod, struck and missed. After recasting (using racing beans once more) I dropped back to sleep and then woke after half an hour to the hissing of foil on the right-hand rod. I struck, but in the beginners' fashion, holding the line to stop the run and not being awake enough to slip on the pick-up. This one I hooked and I felt a fast-moving fish bolt down the margins to the right, taking me well under the trees and, by the feel of it, through some snags. When he'd stopped running, I got the pick-up on and got a proper hold on things. I eased the fish back through the snag, but then he turned and charged off again. It seemed a long time coming, in the misty darkness, with a nasty grating sensation on the line, but at least with a bit of toing and froing and not a complete jam-up. Suddenly I had him free and, in the gloom, saw a dark shape approaching on the surface. Was it the carp? Or was it all weed and twigs? In went the net, there was a splash and out came an amazing carp. As lean as a barbel, about twenty-six inches long and only 8lbs in weight. Huge tail and fins. I put him in the sock and had just rebaited when I heard the scream of a centre-pin. There was a splash and another scream and I jumped over the fence and hurried down to where the dark shape of Trott was crouched by the water, his old dapping rod bent over and a carp running him into the branches on his right. He got him clear after a while and, after a bit of a slog in front of us I reached out and lifted up the mesh round a five-pounder. After sacking that one we made a celebration pot of tea and, while we were drinking it, Lawrence arrived. By the time we'd finished our cups and our conversation, a dull light was glowing in the east and the swallows were twittering somewhere above us. We began to fish again, but though I'd predicted more sport, nothing came to our baits through the dawn and though carp tried desperately to suck down corn through the weedbeds on the far bank, they didn't succeed. We photographed the two carp. Trott put his back first and it sailed out over my left-hand bait and picked it up. The line began to go – Trott struck, I played the fish in. It was only when we had it on the bank that we realised what'd happened.

Thursday 30th – The Wells

Only at the last minute did I decide to go to the Wells. I was going elsewhere, but I'd left it too late and, anyway, it felt a promising evening for those canny carp. Thought, from the amount of cars in the car park, that the pool was going to be crowded, but I laughed to myself as I discovered that the car-owners were either trout anglers or walkers. However, there was one angler at the carp pool, and he was precisely in the spot I wished to fish.

But he was a decent sort of bloke and after a friendly chat I almost forgave him. I went down to the Beech Bough, the one by the overspill, and I completely forgave him. Dark shapes were cruising through the green reflections and one or two of them broke the mirror-like surface lazily sucking down certain tasty morsels. I scattered more offerings and was pleased to see the carp gently and unhurriedly mop them up.

I'd forgotten my crust and only had a box of cat biscuits. But the carp were taking them. My only fear was that they took a while to soak and soften up and I could imagine an impatient fish taking a bait that was too hard to strike a hook through. Yet, unlike other occasions, when carp have been close and taking confidently, I baited up without that nervous excitement that comes from the half-hope of hooking a fish. I wasn't half-hopeful, I wasn't even *full* of hope, I was almost as sure as I could be that today I'd break this season's Wells duck. What's more, I noticed the calmness in the scene and the way it affected me, storing me with a solid confidence. Every cast went out gently and accurately and when a carp heaved up the surface into a bulge, just beyond the rod-tip, I knew the bait was going to be taken. There was a swirl – a slow one – then another bumping of the surface. The line slipped out of my gentle grip between thumb and forefinger and I tapped home the hook.

Splash! The centre-pin whirred and the 'Beauty'

curved into a nice bend. The carp bolted out a few yards, then dived and bored deeply, coming round in an arc to the right and not heading left towards the snags as I'd expected. He plunged about near the surface and I wound him towards me. The strong rod was holding him easily and with 8lb line I seemed to be having everything my own way. I stepped back for the net and then pushed it gently under the water. The fish didn't like it when I tried to draw him over it, he bolted and went deep, curving to the left this time. Hard side-strain, the rod bent-double, swung the carp round and it changed tactics and ran to the right. Again I held him off and the rod went over and slowly came back up as the fish gave in and came back to the surface. I wound down and shortened the line, then drew him over the net. As I lifted he thrashed and splashed, but he was safely enmeshed and soon lying still on the bank, beneath the trees.

A beautiful carp. Deep mahogany flanks and dark blue back, large and perfect fins and tail. Just under 8lbs, and I couldn't help chortling to myself. It was as satisfying as any twenty-pounder from Redmire.

Friday 31st – Sheepwash

Arrived at the pool at about 8.30pm, in torrential rain. Trott wasn't there, which was just as well, as without, at least, a decent brolly, he'd have been drowned. As it was, two young eel-fishers were driven early home and even with the bivouac I was decidedly uncomfortable and wet. Couldn't set the rods up for nearly two hours, during which time I just sat and drank tea, avoiding drips from the leaking canvas. After I'd cast out two baits into the Sticks I tried to get comfortable in the sleeping bag (the old one) and failed.

AUGUST

Saturday 1st

Lawrence arrived at 2.30pm and he had a cup of tea with me as the rain began again. He set up by the willow and I fell back into a damp, fitful sleep. A lightning flash woke me at dawn and I counted the distance to the thunder. Three miles. It came nearer. The dim grey light was suddenly shot through with bright yellow and the crash rolled away for minutes in every direction. At least there wasn't the expected downpour, just a short, sharp shower. When it was light enough to see, I rebaited and recast. The storm cloud suddenly bellowed at me from behind – and I'd thought it had been long gone! But it was just a last word.

I'd had a short run in the night, though nothing that I could hear. Lawrence came round for another cup of tea and I said the morning, which was still mild, was ideal for a carp. Yet I couldn't understand how neither of us had had a decent chance yet.

Lawrence moved round to the corner, I put on a ¼oz bomb and cast for an extravagant bubbler. Lawrence had a carp bite through his line!

With not a twitch to show for my efforts, I went, *sans* rod, down for a second look at the shallow, weedy end and was overjoyed to see not one, but three carp feeding on the surface in the weedbeds and on the farm bank. Quickly, I nipped back for the Fifty-One Slayer and, after losing my last Purina biscuit, cast a maple-flavoured sliver of crust for a surface slurping fish. He was in a small patch of weed and I overcast and drew the crust into it. He found it and spent a few tense minutes pondering over it. Another carp was feeding more enthusiastically in the next weedbed and, as soon as Indecisive had finally decided to play it safe, I moved round to the next pitch where I had only a few yards to cast to the brazen beauty. The carp was feeding in the middle of a big, thick tangle of stems and I waited till its head was up before overcasting, then drawing smoothly (and quite obviously) back until the small piece of crust was right on the smacking lips. I expected the fish to shy away from such reckless tactics, but, instead, the head reached up and immediately took the crust down. There was a wobble on the water as the carp sank and the line twitched once and tightened across the surface. I struck and felt a solid, welcome resistance. Immediately, the fish bolted away to my left, deep under the weeds. Two other fish, unnoticed up till then, also bolted. I whistled for the net as the carp reached open water and dived again, making the Ambidex buzz. The line was tight through the hole in the weed where the fish had gone down and I could feel it wasn't going to clear. I had that unsavoury sensation of line rubbing and pulling through a mass of unyielding stems. I stopped the fish and eased it back into the weeds, he bolted for the bushy margins but, somehow, the pressure from the awkward angle held him off. Invisibly he came up hard into the knot of weed and though he bounced back once, when he came back a second time, there wasn't even a tremor on the line. I even slacked off, but I felt nothing, when I tightened up, but a dead weight.

Lawrence (finally) arrived, puffing and panting and I just kept a steady pressure on, swinging the angle of the line from left to right and sensing that I was beginning to work the weed mass free of its anchoring roots. Suddenly a great section, five by five feet, began to come slowly towards us. But there was no sign of the carp and suddenly I thought I must have lost it. The weed clump came under the bank and Lawrence pushed his net under it. A big golden fish suddenly appeared and shot off to our right. I was thankful that the line was strong and sound and that there was a fraction of give in the weeds, otherwise I'd have lost my carp then. It ploughed around, like a dog tied to a post, and I wished I was able to get direct contact with it. Playing it through the weed-mat was like fighting someone through a mattress. Lawrence pulled some of the weed clear and I brought the fish back to the lessened pile of greenery. It all just about fitted into the landing-net. A big-headed, long-bodied 'wild' mirror of 9lbs. Perfect condition and with huge pectorals and tail.

Lawrence left soon after that little victory. I should've gone too, but I went back to the weedbeds to discover the carp still surface-feeding, and after a cautious and heart-stopping series of casts, I drew the bait over a bubbling mouth and again was rewarded with an instant take. But I was too eager and after a second, waiting for the line to tighten, I decided it wasn't going to and struck. Miles too soon – the fish had only just got it below the surface and hadn't yet taken it properly. It bolted when I struck, thinking, no doubt, that it must have been his lucky day to come across such a dumb angler.

Sunday 2nd – Redmire

Arrived at around seven on a bright, warm evening. As I opened the gate by the oaks, I spotted a movement on the glassy surface and, as I watched, a dark shape cruised into the corner of the dam. This was the first time I've seen a carp in there this season – so I quickly rolled the van under the trees and got out a rod. The carp, sensing my arrival (or more probably *seeing* the van in the sunlight) moved out. Next time I'll leave the van in the hollow, or p'raps I'll have painted it khaki by then. I did, in fact, drive out of the trees and put it in the hollow – but more of an afterthought, this – and too late.

As the sun went down so the carp moved up to the shallows and I was surprised, yet pleased to find the top end of the pool weedier than I've seen it in previous years. In fact it was so thick-grown there were only a few holes to put a bait in – but with such abundant cover, surely even the old Redmire aristocracy would feel secure.

I sneaked up to the willow roots, with the 'B.B.' and a beautiful new centre-pin that was also given to me by Lawrence – five-inch diameter, light, ball-race, ear-boggling check and finished in a dark gunmetal grey. The best thing about it is its mysterious source – no inscription of any kind – probably made about thirty to forty years ago as one of a small number – or it could even be the only one of its kind. I'd had a bit of agonising when I took the now trusty and well-liked Eagle from the rod and replaced it with this 'gun-carriage' of a reel. I tied a 4 Speedbarb on to the 10lb line – when of course I should've tied on a Mustad.

Under the willows, as the sun sloped to the edge of the recently cropped field of rye grass, I dropped a bunch of (red) maggots into a gap in the weeds and watched as the first slow humpings began to rock the glass calm water.

A carp came very near the opening, humped under a

patch of weed, then moved away. But, sure enough, he returned and my heart began to pound as the fish stopped over the bait. The loose line lay on the weed-mat. A patch of bubbles rose from the clearing. For a few moments of fever the carp fed on the loose maggots – but then he ambled away, making shallow ripples and pushing aside the floating scum.

I had to sit down after that! I'd been almost certain he was going to take.

I saw the white reflection of the new moon on the pale surface, where it wasn't rocked by moving carp. An hour almost after sunset and they were there in numbers. One or two had swept casually under the weeds, directly below the rod point, swirling the green mats so that they opened and closed like sea anemones. A fish moved through the weeds to my right and I reeled in the bait and dropped it in a tiny hole, not twelve feet away. There were some bubbles, then the carp moved away, humping beneath the weeds. But the humping went round in a circle and came back to the small gap. I knew, then, he'd seen the bunch of maggots, and I was positive he was going to take. The loose line began to slide gently away across the weed; in the half-light I saw it clearly as it drew slowly – very slowly – and slithered down the hole. I struck and a great weight slammed at the rod. The big reel whirred, with my finger hard on the rim. Gdoosh! Away went a large wave, straight across the shallows.

I kept the rod over to the right and then slipped the check on, fumbling a bit, and the reel literally howled.

It was a big fish, going fast and powerfully in a dead straight line through the dense weed-growth. It was accelerating, rather than slowing.

Then came that terrible hollowness. The line was still tight into the weed, but the run had stopped. There was a second great plunging splash, that panicked another fish, and a big bow wave went curving away across the shallows. There was a faint blue gleam on its smooth crest.

I reeled in a load of weed and there was the bloody pathetic hook – bent open like a forced hinge, gaped open like a vacant expression on an idiot's face. I was the idiot. Not only had I not used a Mustad, I hadn't even tested this ancient Speedbarb – a golden rule broken. Now I knew why I'd had so much misgiving about changing reels – the hook on the Eagle's line was a tried and proven one and I think it would've held even this trial. But the line was only 8lb and then, of course, that would've probably failed me. Similar empty arguments raged within as I strode out from under the willows and swore heartily at my own incompetence.

The moon was going down, pale orange now, and the light was fading. But there was enough afterglow to tie a hook by and I soon had a Mustad on the line and so recast into the weedbeds. Carp were still moving, but, even though I had one go down right beneath the rod again, I was drained and I didn't imagine I'd get another chance. After all my optimism of the last few days this mood was foul medicine. From benign to malign, a demon found me and mashed up my line and made sure my cast went wrong. I laughed in the end and went off to sit in the pump house, making tea by candlelight and undoing the knot that had formed down my throat.

Monday 3rd – The Evening Pitch

A rat rustling in the dry leaves jerked me awake, thinking my silver foil was whispering to me of carp.

It was a dim, misty dawn and the pool was white. The sun was almost up and I got out of my sleeping bag and went for a sneak up to the shallows. Not a thing. Took some pictures of the dawn on my walk around the pool. One or two fish rolled out under the mist.

In the end I got back into my bag and went off to sleep again! Had breakfast at around 10.00am and felt a bit thick in the head – probably through sleeping in the sun. Couldn't find a fish to cast to until around 3.00pm when I dropped a quill in a hole in the weeds and watched a carp ignore the bait. Another, small one, took the bait, but ejected it instantly. And after that no other fish came near. Went on up to the Bale Pitch and tried for a few carp (juniors) up there, but failed. I'm going to resist opening a tin of 'yellow peril' until later – I can't believe my red-for-danger maggots can fail.

All day I was waiting for evening and yet when it came I suddenly felt pessimistic. Fight it, old lad, fight it! But even the small carp were eluding me and as I went back to the willow-roots, having spotted a hefty ripple spreading from under the branches, I slipped on the soft bank and a great fish drifted unhurriedly away from the same place I'd hooked the big one yesterday. I watched a trail of tiny bubbles forming across the shallows, rising up as the carp's fat belly slid through the silt.

The moon appeared again, the crescent a little thicker and higher than before. It deepened in colour from yellow to orange and then, just before it set, red. By then it was dark and though big fish were moving elsewhere, there'd only been one or two drift past me. A few whoppers had leapt, right up at the head of the pool. But, with the thick mats of weed and only the few clear holes between, it was futile to cast after dark.

My silver paper twitched and even as I struck I knew what I'd got. A nasty little eel.

Tuesday 4th

The 'Open' Pitch. 'Open' is a joke, with all the willow and alder branches hanging about my head. It's time this pitch was given a real name. Woke after sunrise on a white dawn. Thick mist over the land and pool, heavy dew. It was like an early autumn dawn rather than a high summer morning. Very quiet and saw little activity on my morning round. Naturally, the baits hadn't been touched. But I felt much more optimistic – there was a feel in the air and a look to the water that stored me with hope. I'm not saying more than that, just yet. All I'll add is that I've decided to fish Ingham's tonight and that, come this evening, I'll bait up the area in front of Wasp Island with macaroni, fishing that with one rod and maggot with another.

Spent the day away from the pool, exploring the Wye Valley and visiting a cool church – it was the only cool place in the district. When I got back, I made tea and had it on the elm-stump, watching the evening coming on. Then I crept up to the shallows and cast for some carp up at Quinlan's. But they were very wary and moved off after a while.

From Wasp Island, I cast my macaroni right next to one or two feeding fish. These carp went right over the bait, bubbling well, and the line never moved. So I changed from macaroni and maggot and, as the light began to fade, hooked a nice eel.

I went round to the Bale Pitch as the carp had moved away from the island. I put out two maggot-baited hooks and then sat back on the comfortable seat (a hay bale) to wait. Just as the reddening moon was sinking into the haze behind me, I had a twitchy bite on the right-hand rod and struck quickly, feeling sure this was an eel. Luckily, I missed. I couldn't see clearly enough to recast, so I just sat behind the one rod – the old Walker Avon. After a few minutes I had a twitchy draw – the silver paper flickering to the butt-ring. Bloody eel, I thought, striking half-heartedly. There was a great splash and the rod wound over. The clutch buzzed and the fish that wasn't an eel bolted into the weedbeds. Bloody hell! It felt good too. There was another surge and a big splash. Then everything stopped and for a second I thought it was off – but I felt a tremor coming down the line. The rotten, stinking net had tangled in a bramble stem and I frantically tried to unhitch the knotted-up mesh. I just kept the line taut as I held on to rod and net with both hands. The line went slack. I tightened up; it went slack again. O, curse! He's off. I wound in a mass of weed, sliding it across the margins and then bending down to shake it clear of the hook. It exploded! The carp was diving and breaking the line before I could slack it off. It could've broken the rod-top if I'd been on a short length. However, I'm sure he hadn't been a real biggun – but even so I was suitably rankled. I'd even tried to get him with the net after he'd snapped me and my desperate lunge broke the screw out of the pole. What a mess! It seemed so catastrophic, I ended up roaring with laughter and frightening the coots. Still, it was better than crying.

Wednesday 5th

I *wasn't* going to have a blank and I went up this morning armed with the Avocet and Eagle, a combination that sounds interesting and feels just right. There were carp by the Bale Pitch again – not big ones it's true – but carp. I cast out a just-made crow-quill float and two grains of 'consistency' and after I'd put it in the gap in the weeds where I wanted it, I sat back in the hazy sunshine to enjoy the warm morning.

A carp came under the float, hovered, and moved off. Another followed in a few minutes and bolted from the area. But there was still another carp, feeding on the loose grain and I saw the quill shudder and lift, then twitch and begin to slide away. I struck and the Avocet went over into a hoop. It was a spirited tussle. In and out of the weedbed, the reel rasping, then the fish coming in and wallowing a bit before I could slide him over to me. Got it by hand (I'd left the net behind!). A lovely three-penny-bit of a common – just over 5lbs. Blank saved.

There was quite a bit of activity in the weedbed and big fish constantly jostled the surface as they basked in the heat of the sun. But, apart from a bit of crust, I had nothing that would've interested them. However, I didn't offer the crust, which was very unenterprising of me.

Went up to the Arms at lunchtime. Had a doze under the willows when I came back. Dave and a fellow farm-worker came down to cool themselves with a wash below the overspill. It was so hot, every movement had to be slow and unhurried. Went down to Llangarren for pro-vision and Clare had sent me a lovely card to collect from the Post Office. Had tea and then moved up to Green-banks, standing in the mass of flowering willowherb and casting to big, slow-cruising fish, who were obviously stopping to feed on the loose grains of corn. As the lazy turbulence unfurled over the bait, I imagined the conse-quences of the hoped-for run. The line would slide off across the surface and the strike would send a big fish charging away into the dense weeds, the rod weighed down further and further with each thrust of the tail. But the line stayed loose from the tip and the carp slowly drifted away.

I stayed for some time in the willowherb, while the carp moved nearby. But after half an hour or so they were definitely moving out of the area, so I went up to the willow roots and put out two baits into the weeds.

A dark cloud had reached up, like a finger, across the sun and as its hard outline broke up it spread across from the sky and the evening quickly darkened. Within minutes there were drops of rain falling on the calm pool.

Couldn't be better, I thought. I'd prayed for rain and got it. Yet as it increased I realised I'd have to get my canvas up for the night. That was a bother; I didn't want to disturb the evening's fishing. But the rain got heavier and put an end to my stalking anyway.

I cleared a space in the Fence Pitch and set up the bivouac. As the rain poured down on the canvas I lit a candle and the stove and made tea. It was just like old times. Rain hammering, tea by candlelight, and a few hours to read or write.

Thursday 6th

There was rain in torrents in the night and distant rolls of thunder. At 6.30am I made some tea and then went out into the dark grey morning to see what was moving. I'd heard continued splashings and rollings at one pause in the night's rainstorm and obviously the carp had been up in the shallows in numbers. What I pity I hadn't set up another big brolly and sat it out until morning – it would've been only until morning as there wasn't a fish in sight at 7.00am. But it looked very promising elsewhere – the temperature was still quite warm and the heavy sky looked as if it was going to stay that way.

I recast and a fish rolled right in front of me, only thirty feet away. But even so, it was natural for most of the activity to be over on the west bank! There! A fish has just rolled again – just off Keffords. I think I'll have to take a stroll around in a while and drive them back over here.

* * *

I did take a stroll – with a rod – bloody hell! There were carp in the margins of the Willow Pitch and that's the first time I've seen them there for years. They began to feed almost immediately on the couple of handfuls of maggots I threw in. But the only bite I got produced a wretched eel. The flurry of action put the carp down, so I went on and found a carp feeding on surface-weed off the platform – just like a Sheepwash fish. I went and got some crust, but as I prepared to cast, the carp submerged and disappeared. I wasted half an hour waiting for it to return. It did, in fact, come back to the surface – but a long way from my crust. I realised that I'd been wasting valuable time when I climbed the island tree and looked out. I've never seen anything like it. There must've been fifty carp, all big and all feeding madly. There were great clouds of mud and bubbles and dark shapes cruised by beneath me, dipping down every so often for some titbit or other. Quickly, I set up rods on the island. One fishing corn over in weedbed and one with free-lined maggots (God, how I wish I'd remembered more plasticine – I was nearly out of my meagre supply). I might as well not have bothered with two rods. The carp were feeding well on maggots but they never even looked at the corn.

In the dim light of midday, with the clouds as thick as night, the eels were unusually active. I caught two and I knew the carp didn't like it as the little writhers were hauled out from under their noses. I got a third, finicky eel-type bite and, in my annoyance, pulled the line back, hoping to scare it off the bait. There was a huge swirl and a tug and a nice carp bow-waved off. Bloody fool! I swore into the drizzling rain.

I was just going to recast when I noticed the dark shape of a big carp right below the rod-tip. I just dropped the bunch of maggots in front of his nose. For a few minutes he never moved and I began to think that I was wrong, that because of the low light I'd mistaken a clump of weed for a fish; but then it very slowly moved forward, tilting down as it did so. I held my breath. The line twitched as it hung between rod-tip and surface. Then it began to tighten and, as the rod was still in my hands, I just gave a little tug. There was a great clumping splash. The rod heaved forward almost horizontally as the carp surged out from under the tree and made a huge bow wave that headed towards the far bank. It didn't quite make that extreme distance because of the weedbeds which eventually brought it to a clogged stop. For several fraught minutes I simply held tight, hoping the fish would gradually uncork itself. I couldn't change the angle of the line because I was stuck on the island but, inch by inch, constant pressure finally brought the carp up to the surface sixty yards out. There was another great splash, another plunge away and then the line went horribly slack. I reeled in to find the hook still there and undamaged, but I didn't feel like casting again. The carp had been clearly visible for just a split second after I first connected. It was a plum-coloured mirror and it looked at least 30lbs.

I trudged drippily back to my camp, made a last cup of tea, jotted down these notes and then piled all my gear into the van. But I can't quite leave yet. I just want to sit

here (in the van now) watching the water for a few more minutes, as if to say I'm really perfectly happy just being here, whether I catch a fish or not. But that would be a lie.

Sunday 23rd – Redmire

As you see, the previous fortnight was very quiet on the home front. I did go fishing, but the two short trips I had were not exactly full of drama – though it should be said that driving at speed down a country lane, from a carp pond to The Anglers Rest, with the Chairman of the G.S.C. in the rear-gun position, the flap of the van open and a blowpipe continually pounding the following car, driven by the Rodmaker with the Treasurer accompanying: this can seem quite dramatic. I also had three carp rise for my baits – but all refused. So it was with a happy heart that I returned to this beloved place. Roy was already here, looking as enthusiastic (in his quiet way) as ever.

It was 7.30pm. The sun was already almost balanced on the ridge of the valley. Quickly I set up a rod and went up to the shallows. There were carp everywhere. While I'd been chatting to Roy by the oaks, great swirls had been opening in the weedbeds. Up in the shallows, there were humpings, ripples and slow waves going by me. But I didn't get a chance. P'raps I should've gone round to the north-west bank.

After much messing around, drinking tea and *mixing* (!) bait (that ghastly stuff Rod has convinced me to try) I finally got the rods out at midnight – or just before. I was fishing in the Ash Grove – a convenient spot for the first night – yet … but more of that later. I'd just got into my bag when I heard a steady hiss above the faint trickle of water going over the overspill. Left-hand rod. Whack! Dzzzzzzzz! A satisfactory pull, at speed, from the corner of the dam, round in an arc into the weedbeds in front of me. There was a swirling splash and I whistled to Roy and called him. But he was right up at the top of the pool. All I heard was my own echo, bouncing back from the barns. Ne'er mind. I eased the carp out of the weeds and got the net into the water. Away he went again, the rod throbbing and then slowly nodding as the fish ran, then just hung with his tail working slowly. I got him up to me and saw, in the darkness, the clot of weed on the surface. This black blob began to draw away to the left. I let it go and the clutch buzzed again (I do like the Ambidex 9 – out of all my reels it's the best one for playing big carp). Back came the weed blob and, being very gentle, slow and deliberate, I slid it over the net and hoped the fish was there too when I lifted! It was. Not quite as big as I'd first hoped – and I guessed he was a mid-double. His flanks glowed pale beneath the dark trees.

After I'd put on a new hook (the golden 8 had opened fractionally) and recast (all this was easier said than done) I got back into the sack and slept, fitfully, till morning. Then, of course, I slept deeply – until Roy woke me with a welcome cup of tea. How pleasant. Tea in bed on the banks of Redmire, on a fine summer morning. He'd had a couple of brief chances in the night, but he wasn't given long enough. I told him about the chance I'd also missed in the night (the paper had risen and I hadn't heard it!) and also about the carp in the sack that had weighed in (by candlelight) at 13lbs. But we didn't get the fish out just then – I wanted the sun to rise higher for its portrait. And also I thought we might get another one and make it a group portrait. But there were no more fish moving and, at about 10.00am, I went to lift the sack out from the dam-rail. The carp wasn't in it! It was like going to pay for a seven-course meal and discovering the notes in the wallet had just flown away by themselves. 'Never mind,' said Roy, 'you'll just have to catch another one the same.'

After 2.00pm – no, before then – clouds began to come over and the hot sun went in. Carp began to go up the pool. It was just like that afternoon in June '77, when I fished with Roy on the first week of the season. Afternoon sessions on the shallows don't happen more than once or twice a season. I went out on to Wasp Island and had carp feeding over a handful of maggots almost instantly. One second to adjust float and plasticine, then out went a gold size 12 with six grubs along the shank.

An hour had almost passed and one or two carp had gone over the bait, but hadn't taken it. Four very large fish had suddenly appeared, over to my left. They didn't stay in those extreme shallows for long though; one came through the mud-cloud the smaller carp had been stirring up – right beneath my crow-quill.

Suddenly, a twenty-pound, fully-scaled mirror appeared, right over the bait. I gawped as the quill stirred and moved to the right – but it was only a momentary touch – the next second, the big fish was pushing away from me, obviously suspicious. As he disappeared into the weeds, another, much smaller fish, came quickly into view, swimming directly towards me and straight over the bait. The white-tipped float sailed away serenely. I jerked the rod-tip and the carp bolted. He went more powerfully than I expected for such a modest-sized fish. As he plunged into the weedbed, forty feet away, I wondered whether he might be bigger than the 8–9lbs I'd guessed him at. That first rush didn't even give me time to put on the check of the Gun Carriage. I clicked it home and it raged angrily as the carp made a desperate lunge to my left, shooting through the weeds and then suddenly coming to a halt.

Roy, fishing in the Fifty-One pitch opposite, had been watching the commotion. Now he came running with a net as I drew the fish back to the island. He came in fairly quietly and Roy slipped the mesh under a beautiful common of exactly 13lbs. It was almost identical in shape to the one I'd had last night – except that the dorsal wasn't so pronounced. I secured the sack properly this time and went back to the shallows to see if I could make it a double. I nearly made it a great double! A common of around 20lbs took my bunch of maggots in his stride and the quill slid away again. A big wave went down the pool until, suddenly, that groan-inspiring sensation. I reeled up to discover the small hook had snapped on the bend. FAKKS! Needless to say I changed to a 10, even though I'm sure the hook was sound (I feel it was crushed rather than pulled apart). I had to go and have tea after that and by the time the quill was out in the water again, it was getting dark. After about fifteen minutes, just as the float was beginning to shimmer into the gloom, I saw it clearly again, sliding positively to the left. A firm strike, a swirl and then a great splash as the pressure from the rod and the carp's own momentum caused it to aquaplane across the surface. From the timbre of the splash, I knew it wasn't a big fish, but he fought like one – surging back and forth before coming, plunging, into the net and out. 9lbs – a very solid, dark coloured common, but more streamlined in shape than the 13.

I cast out two balls of seafood bait from the corner of the dam and spent the night there.

Tuesday 25th

It was so hot and quiet, we went up to Llangrove to enjoy a cool pint at the Arms. In the farmyard behind the pub there was a big pig sleeping in the sun. It looked just like a flat, pink rock and for the duration of our lunch break, it never even twitched an ear. Roy was having to leave today and as he hadn't yet even hooked a carp, he was determined to have a final fling on the shallows. I sat with him, up behind the willow logs in the Fifty-One pitch, as carp up to around 18lbs mooched about in front of us. The afternoon became overcast and it seemed perfect for the prospect of it. I also showed great restraint, sitting with him for nearly three hours while the carp were feeding and not mucking things up by going on to the opposite bank and perhaps hooking one immediately. (Bloody big head.) At 6.00pm he gave up, having had three narrow misses. He was exhausted and needed his tea. I felt the same and put out two chairs in the corner of the dam while the kettle boiled.

After he'd gone, waving a cheery goodbye despite his blank, I felt as if some of my hope had gone with him. A curious thing to think, especially when I consider how much I love my solitude: but, without doubt, there are times when I fish much more confidently and positively when I'm fishing with a (quiet) friend, especially an optimistic friend, like Henry. I didn't get the chance I thought I'd get, up on the shallows.

Wednesday 26th

An uneventful night, though I heard one or two fish leaping far up the pool. I'd been unbelievably slovenly and hadn't moved pitch, as I'd said I would. It was easier to stay where I was. (And I've only got a sleeping bag and the rods to move.)

Creeping along the bank at about 9.00am I heard two coots fighting over by Keffords. I glanced across and saw a big bow wave shoot out from the bank. Aha! With rod and maggots, I went round the lake and, sure enough, there were a number of good fish right in the margins. A cluster of bubbles sparkled brilliantly in the strong, facing sunlight. I got down in the willowherb between Keffords and the Stile and cast from there. The carp moved over the baited area and hovered over the bait. I watched the tiny star in the water that was the point where the line cut through the surface tension. But the star never moved.

As I was facing the sun, it was difficult to see clearly and also I soon got very hot. The carp began to drift away into deeper water. Tried, in the afternoon, for a small fish on the shallows; had one bite in a hole in the duck-weed. Missed it.

Another golden sunset, which promised yet more golden sunsets. The wind is in the north – except the wind never blows. At last I moved across to a new pitch and cast out two rods from the Stile. Then, after two welcome mugs of dry cider (it had been another scorcher), I lay back on the bank and gazed up at the shroud of stars. It was an hour before I fell asleep.

Thursday 27th

I woke to the steady hiss of a duet for silver paper – that is, two on a line, not one on each line.

'What's going on?' I said, as I reached forward and made a ridiculous strike. I didn't hit it hard enough or wait for the line to tighten. I blame the hypnotic stars and the two mugs of cider. A hefty blow hit the rod-top and, as it went over, I prepared for a godalmighty rush. It never came. The hook-hold went. Serve it right for not being caught. Fancy disturbing my sleep like that!

I woke again, just as the first blue haze was beginning to dim the brightness of the crescent moon. There was a light mist sweeping across the pool and the foil on the Mk IV was jammed in the butt-ring. Curses. I spent ten minutes of slow hauling, during which time I must've retrieved ten feet of line! Something was there, but coming through dense weed only grudgingly. I decided to hand line and my steady pull soon broke the line at the loop of the braided trace. Though I pouted a bit, I feel sure now that I'd got a big eel on the end. The run had only taken a yard or two, and I hadn't heard it, probably because it just twitched slowly out, à la eel.

I went to the pump house to make up another trace and boil a kettle for tea. (I haven't mentioned the traces, have I? Masterline sent me 100yds of Black Dacron, 15lb b.s., just when I'd convinced myself that braided nylon probably did have an advantage over ordinary line. I'd hooked every carp so far, this week, on yard hook-lengths of the stuff and, certainly, after the way the fish had avoided my baits last time, this week's observations and catches have proved the difference between presentation on the wiry mono and then on these supple lengths of the braid.)

When I got back to the Stile, the sun was just beginning to cast its beams through the mist, as the valley edge tilted across its bright face. I catapulted maggots into two other areas of water to my left and, after an hour, with the sun becoming quite warm, the first bubbles and swirls were beginning to break over the baited pitches. I fished from behind the willowherb – in the same place as yesterday. Only this time I used the mesh of a landing net to unroll the coils of line from my big centre-pin. Casting went much better and smoother.

After a while, with the float under a bit of pressure from surface drift, I saw two dark shapes much closer than where I'd cast to. So, very gently, I eased the quill back until it was in the area of water only twenty feet from the bank. A minute passed, then the white tip of the float just sank, slowly and deliberately, sliding away from me at the same time. I struck and a wave zoomed out, heading out towards the Fence opposite and to the left. Forty yards whizzed off the reel before I put the check on.

I stopped the carp and there was a swirl, then the reel screamed as the fish dived and headed right for a few yards. I felt the curious sensation of friction as the rough texture of the trace cut through the water. The rod hard over and my left hand firmly on the drum of the Gun Carriage; the fish shot into the bank, thirty-five yards up the pool.

I was standing in the margins, the net at the ready, when the fish swirled and rolled and came in front of me. I could see now his modest proportions and was amazed at his power. He churned about strongly for another few minutes before I finally eased him over the net.

He'd given as good a performance as any fish twice his size. He weighed 9¼lbs!

Nothing stirred on the pool for about four or five hours after that. But then carp began to head up towards the shallows – only a few, yet some big ones amongst them. I'd thought this might happen, as I sat in supreme luxury on the overspill, watching the way the wind was turning. As I sipped my tea, sitting in a comfortable camp chair, basking in the sun, I noticed ripples heading away from me and the breeze was westerly for the first time this week (I threw some crusts off the dam and a fish swirled at them).

Eventually, after having to make a couple of calls from the village, I crept on to the island at the pool's head and flicked out my float tackle. After half an hour a superb, dark-looking common of around 25lbs glided out of the weeds and passed about forty feet from me. It turned towards the float and for a tense moment I thought everything had begun to swing my way. But everything missed me by about four feet – I almost felt a draught of fins as the big carp went by.

It was obviously going to be a good evening. I should have tea now, while the sun was still high, and then bring back a second rod and some of Rod's Special. So off I went and put my chair on the dam and had tea and cake, looking expectantly up the length of the pool.

Every few minutes I glanced over my left shoulder to see how low the sun was sinking. It didn't seem to sink at all. Tea over, I put on a darker shirt and took a pullover with me in case the evening cooled. Then, with the old Avon and the necessary blowpipe, I went back up to Wasp Island. There was a carp feeding on the maggots I'd put out before I left. I hardly dared breathe, let alone cast, as it was a good fish, and there were other, bigger ones nearby. Eventually I swung the maggot-baited float-tackle out – though it didn't go out as neatly as I wished. Then, in slow motion, I inserted a rod-rest into the bank, laid the Avon in it, loaded the pipe with the hook-bait and fired it across to the willow opposite. It went out as neatly as anyone could wish – and no angler living could've achieved that with a normal, underhand cast – it was not only too far to cast normally, but the branches made even underhand casts impossible. I 'piped' free samples around the hook-bait.

Humping ripples broke up the reflections and I watched obviously big carp come right over the blow-piped area. Then a fish of around 15lbs came up to the maggots and right below the float. The quill shuddered but then the carp swam off, obviously suspicious. Nothing came back to the float, though numbers of carp were passing over the other 'hot' spot. I waited expectantly for the line to slide across the surface – but it didn't.

Under the oaks, I had my nightcap of cider, watching the last light fade on the surface. The evenings seem so short now, compared to the lingering hours of twilight in June and July. One minute the sun has been balanced on the far hills, then, before I'd had time to think, everything is disappearing into the dusk. As the blue haze diminished in the west I went round to the Stile – where the crickets were chirruping in the dry grass – and put out three baits in the open water between the bank and the weedbed, sixty yards away.

Friday 28th

Woke a few hours later to that heart-jolting sound. The line was streaming out and this time I struck firmly after the proper interval. What happened?! No, I hadn't missed. As I reeled in what I thought was a slack line, a thrumming weight began to bend the rod. A bloody eel – a big one too. It went round the line of the right-hand rod and tied it into a neat eel basket. Luckily, the monster was only lightly hooked and I managed to force a separation within a few seconds. But it took me half an hour to sort out the subsequent mess. As I did so, I listened to the continued distant crashes and plunges. The carp were still up in the shallows, feeding like billy-o, from the sound of it. But I was too exhausted by my sore trial with the eel, and also suddenly very cold. I'd been too warm to begin with, but now the 4.00am chill was seeping through to me. I gave up on the still-tangled rods and fished with just one. Then I dived back into my bag and fell asleep to the sound of rolling carp. How could I have been so pathetic?

I woke much too late. The sun was over the trees on the opposite bank and the mists had dispersed. Not a fish anywhere, until I spotted, after breakfast, a group of big commons down by the Willow Pitch. They had an expression about them that reminded me of naughty boys caught stealing apples. Without doubt, they'd been gorging themselves in the night. Guilt was on their faces, though they were trying to appear as aloof as ever; 'What?! Us? On the shallows? Never!' I went up to the shallows and the weedbeds had been smashed into drifting fragments. Stupid, lazy angler. A night's sleep would've been easy to sacrifice – and I may have had something magnificent in return.

Up by the willows, at 11.00am (approx.) there were one or two carp cruising. I spotted a big one. But there was a conspiracy afoot. The cows waded where they'd never waded before, a blackbird flew in a direct line over the browsing fish. The carp bolted for cover, but kept coming back. I cast from Wasp Island and a fish swam straight *into* my quill! When I reeled in, I found the bait had tangled round the line and there was an untidy knot below the float. I bumped into branches I'd always avoided unconsciously before. Things would only get worse if I didn't stop trying. I went home, leaving the pool still and blue under the summer sky.

SEPTEMBER

Wednesday 2nd – Shillinglee

The morning was blue and hazy – the woods were in the distance, like memory. The trees were still, and not a sound of a bird or a sigh of a breeze. I imagined Shillinglee, the great spread of bluish water under a great spread of sky; that was where I should go today, after a very busy forty-eight hours…

But first – breakfast, then a stroll through the woods with Clare, who had the energy of a grasshopper today. It wasn't till four in the afternoon that I was heading south-eastwards. As I drove I sang a foolish song – something about me not being such a berk. It was daft that I'd had some misgivings about a rush of recent work and commitments, especially as I wasn't truly concerned about them. Perhaps it was just a slight feeling of emptiness waiting to be filled again after running around in every direction for miles and miles. But on the green banks of Shillinglee I began to calm. The sun was warm, the sky bright and the trees were still heavy with summer. I walked slowly round the banks, talking to the only angler on the water as he fished from the dam. No, he said, he'd not caught anything, though he was hoping for a rudd or a bream. No, he'd never caught a Shillinglee carp and had only ever heard of one being landed. I went along the wooded western bank, all the time hoping to see a sign that would cause me to thread my line through the rod-rings. Not until I was approaching the lily-covered shallows did I see any fishy movement.

I'd passed two delectable-looking weedy bays where the dark canopy of the oaks shaded the margins (looking out towards the sunlit lake it was as if I was peering out from a cave), and as I came round towards the island I saw a slow ripple about twenty-five yards out. It was obviously a carp, but even though a dark back momentarily broke surface it was difficult to judge its size.

Not far from the boathouse (after discovering the best-looking pitch on the lake, right next to a Burgh Heath-sized willow) I found another carp rooting through a reed bed. I almost set up my tackle, but in the end I was content simply to stand by the water watching the reflected sunset and dreaming up plans for my next visit.

Home for supper, my mind full of glorious imaginings of full moons by that willow tree. I was so fired up that I decided, as I ate my lovely meal with my lovely wife, that

I must soon apologise and sneak out again for a cast. I was gone in half an hour, down to the Wells – but the dark had almost shadowed over in that time. I was caught by the swift-sinking September evening. Red horizon at 8.30. Dark by 9.00. I made just one cast and packed up an hour later, stumbling away from the star-reflecting pool with its mysterious splashes and plops, blundering through the pitch-black wood, barely able to follow the narrow path. But then the trees parted and I could see my way up over the hill, across the cricket field and back down through the next wood to our cottage. How cosy it looked, the lit windows just visible through the black tangle of branches.

No fish, but I was now in good spirits again, as was Clare – high spirits, like a wind blowing the leaves away in autumn.

Autumn – it won't be long now.

Saturday 5th – R. Rother Fittleworth

A sudden urge to fish running water came over me and, after tea, on a warm, blue, typically September evening, I set off for a bit of chubbing.

The light was soft and luminous, and the sun was just beginning to fade when I made my first cast, just upstream of the Pipe. I trotted corn for half an hour, but only got a few twitchy bits. I didn't care; I was in fine form, ready for nothing and the sun went down like a furnace. It was a truly beautiful evening. As soon as the sun had disappeared, a thin blue mist began to rise across the water meadows and the moon, in its first quarter, shone silvery in the south. I took off the float and moved downstream of the Pipe. The river looked so promising – it's the first time I've seen this stretch in its summer clothes. I said as much to another chub-angler (he had *all* the gear) but he scowled and said that nothing had been caught all day. I couldn't believe it. I dropped a 12 hook and two grains of corn into the slack under the bank and a more promising patch of chub-water would be hard to imagine. The line angled tight after a minute, but I missed. Next cast produced a gentle pluck-pluck, which again I missed. Third time lucky. There was a much more positive pull. I followed with the tip for a second, then struck. Aha! Something tugged hard and dived into the bankside reeds. I soon freed it and in a moment or two I had a 1lb chub in the net (lucky the net had a long handle, as I'd never have reached it otherwise). Like last week's fish, this one was taken on a braided cast – 3lb b.s. on a 6lb main line. Also (it sounds as if I've just caught a six-pounder!) I was, for the first time, using the Leney Aerial. Don Leney gave me his superb 1922 centre-pin after I told him how much I admired those reels. Best fish on it so far, a 28lbs Icelandic salmon in 1926! It spins better than a brand new Grice & Young Coq D'or.

Back at the riverside, I moved downstream and was amazed to discover how the Three Fishes had been transformed since I'd last been there. A big weedbed now stretches right down its length – making it a good trotting swim; yet it was almost dark and I could only fish it by casting into the slack below the weeds and putting the rod in a rest. I put foil on the line and it jerked up to the rod after only a few minutes. I struck and missed – and I missed the next one, too.

The field opposite looked as if it was under a snowdrift as the mist thickened in the bright moonlight. A really good night for a chub and I'd have given my old carp rod for a big one in those conditions. But I had no more chances. Home by 10.15pm.

Monday 7th

Wasn't sure where I was going, but thought I'd spend the 'day' on two or p'raps three different waters. First choice was obvious and I was at the Wells just as the midday sky began to darken ominously. Unfortunately, I didn't have the pool to myself, though the two other anglers kept quietly to the lily bank while I kept to the open bank. Back and forth patrolled the carp. A shower of warm rain, the first for a fortnight, got the fish looking hungry and some free crusts went down in the half-hour after the rain had stopped. But not until 4.30pm did I get a chance to put my bait over a carp. It landed gently just beyond it and drifted back towards it. Sure enough, the dark form turned towards it and tilted up its mouth. There was a quick suck, then a quicker ejection. That was my only chance. Chasing carp for five hours was exhausting work and instead of going straight off to another lake, I had to go home for tea.

At 7.00pm, as the sun sank into hazy cloud, I decided go down to Forked Pond. In a way, I had misgivings about it, as the evening was mild and calm and I guessed what might be happening back at the Wells. However, the wide expanse of lily-covered water was a delightful sight after the narrow pool in the shady valley. And straight away I spotted carp – something very large was moving just beneath the surface, right in the near corner. I didn't bother to go stalking – what was the point? I moved along to a gap in the trees and cast next to the lilies. The fish was joined by others and they slowly shadowed first one way, then the other, but never quite came over the baited area (corn).

It was soon dark. The moon shone in the clearing sky and the trees on the nearest point opposite were vividly silhouetted while the rest of the landscape faded into a general haze. I packed up at 9.00pm without having a touch. The derelict house on the edge of the wood glowed eerily in the moonlight.

Tuesday 8th – Forked Pond

Woke at dawn and very nearly got up – but at the last minute, I weakened. It had rained heavily in the night and the morning was overcast and warm – perfect conditions. I boiled up some paprika racing beans and was at the Pond just before 11.30. Had a sneak about with salmon eggs first, having spotted a bubbler. But there seemed not even a feel of carp up in the lily-covered bays – and when I got back to the corner, there was a dark shape gliding in under the ripples.

Though it'd been calm up in the Vale, there was a steady breeze blowing across the wide pond and the First Corner seemed the obvious place to fish as the ripples were chasing straight into it. I'd already sprinkled a few handfuls of racing beans alongside the lilies and I cast out the one lot with the old Walker Avon and the other with the 'B.B.' and Gun Carriage. After only a few minutes, the line on the latter rod tightened and I struck hard – and missed. Not long after there was another tightening of the line, but I missed again. Without doubt, carp were cruising very close to me.

The sun came out of a gap in the billowing cloud and I had my packed lunch and a bottle of Old Peculier. The carp bow-waved through the pads and came quietly out into the open water. Every now and then a shower of bubbles broke surface. Were they taking the bait? I longed for a good solid run and a hefty resistance to the instant strike. The line angled out once more and again I struck – but this was a fish merely cruising between the bait and the bank; a big wave went off when I lifted the rod.

A frog jumped into the water and swam under the rod-tips. Not long after I saw a movement on my left and heard a rustle when I turned. I chased whatever it was and caught it under the bankside bushes – a dark-coloured grass snake. I let him go after admiring him, taking his appearance as a good omen.

Bigger patches of bubbles opened up. The fish *were* feeding on the bait, I was positive. But they were actually nearer than the hook baits. I watched the water furling and billowing only ten feet from the tip of the Avon. When the disturbance had stopped and the fish moved on, I tossed out a handful of beans and then rebaited with two on the size 10. I flicked it out only a few yards from the bank, close to an overhanging alder branch (after taking off most of the plasticine 'ledger').

I'd had the lake to myself all day, but, at about 4.00pm, another fisherman arrived. He talked, quietly, with me for a while. 'A 25lb common was caught two weeks ago,' he said. 'Superb!' I said. 'That's what *I'd* like; a 20lb common from a local water.'

He wandered off after half an hour and within minutes of his departure the little scrap of foil on the Avon flicked across to the butt-ring and the line flew off the reel. I struck and was straight into a magnificent resistance. *Two* bow waves shot out from the trees. The one I was directly involved with powered away parallel with the right-hand bank and through the big lily bed. The Ambidex kept up a steady Dzzzzzzzzzzzzzzzzzzzzzzzz zzzzzzzzzzzzzzzzzzzzzzzzzzzzzzzzzzzzzzzzzzzzzzzzzzzzz – just as the carp reached the limit of his run – about thirty-five yards into the pads. He rolled and plunged and bolted a few yards to the left. Bubbles rose between the plate-sized leaves as I eased the fish back. He thrashed and dived again, boiled about, then, just when I thought he was surrendering, he sounded and stuck.

I held the rod high and watched the line as it angled down into a clump of pads at the near edge of the vast bed. From that knotted pile of stems and leaves, it stretched away under the mass of treacherous-looking surface growth. It seemed as if I might be gaining a yard or two, but it was only the pressure straightening out the line as it lay, zigzagged between the stems.

Knowing this was a good fish, I didn't want to risk forcing it and wasn't sure whether my chances were good or bad; it's been years since I had a big fish in the lilies and I'd forgotten what it felt like. Needing some encouragement, I whistled loudly to the other angler and told him I'd hooked a decent fish which was now stuck in the pads. He hurried over to me, and then said: 'What do you suggest?' I gave him a quick look and laughed. He probably thought that I meant he should wade out with the net! A bow wave appeared on the surface, between the pads and for an 'orrible moment I thought the fish was off and gone. But there'd been no last lunge on the line. I was still attached to a dead weight. 'I might try slackening off, but I'm loath to do it.' A few minutes passed and I suddenly said: 'I don't know whether he's still there,' and lowered the rod at the same time. I felt a delicious tremor as the fish backed off. I immediately tightened up again and the old Avon must've been truly doubled as I piled on pressure. Much further than I'd imagined, a great shower of bubbles burst into the sunlight and spread across the surface. It was as if we were looking at a great tiled floor covered with bright ball bearings. O, joy! He was moving again. A tail showed above the pads. As it slapped down I shifted the brute a yard, wound down and gently heaved again. There was a gradual, grudging, losing of ground and with every inch I gained I felt a weight lifting from me.

'I don't like the look of that,' said my gillie, pointing to the great knot of stems and leaves, through which, like a needle's eye, the line was stretching.

'Nor me. I'll be glad when I get him clear. The most satisfying sensation in the world is when you draw a snagged fish back into open water!'

Round the knot of lilies he plunged and wallowed, sometimes showing a broad back, sometimes a black tail. I'd said he wasn't very big, to calm myself, and though my gillie seemed to agree, I knew this was the biggest fish of the season. To my great relief, he didn't suddenly jam at the edge of the pads. He rolled and floundered and the pressure on the rod told me I was still winning, still in direct contact. Then he was clear, wallowing on the surface ten yards out. My gillie crouched low, the net held deep in the water. The carp lunged from side to side, but on the tight line, he couldn't get his head down and kept rolling back to the surface. I stepped back a few yards and just drew the fish towards the net. The last seconds, when the carp seemed huge but still remote, ticked away without mishap. The gillie, who'd obviously done this sort of thing before, waited until the bulk of the fish was right between the arms before smoothly lifting. I nearly fell over when I realised it was safe and the battle won.

I put the rod down and went to have a look. 'He's there!' said the gillie, meaning he was over 20lbs.

Not only was he 'there', he was also a common!

We laid him on the bankside path and his dark copper scales gleamed at their gold edges. He was a real tub of a carp, not as gross as a gutty mirror, but very broad and deep. I thought he might just scrape the mark, but the pointer on the clock balance registered 27lbs 11oz. I couldn't believe it and took over the weighing myself. As soon as I'd got hold of the weighing bag I knew the reading was accurate. However, we put it on my brass balance to confirm it and, sure enough, the weight was nearly 27¾ – ½lb for the bag. So I called it 27-3. After a few photographs, we released him in deep water. Then I packed up and was home in time for tea.

Afterwards, I went down to Sheepwash to spend the evening fishing and talking with Lawrence. He took his hat off when I told him about the big common! (No, I think it flew off by itself.) Anyway, neither of us had a run, though Lawrence had had an amazing time there last Sat. evening. Lots of runs and two carp – best 12lbs. Best Sheepwash fish for five years.

Wednesday 9th – Forked Pond

Went back for a couple of hours on a warm, calm evening. The carp were moving in the corner, again, some coming right beneath the leaf raft under the bank. I didn't get a touch, though I saw carp cruising over the baited area. My 'gillie' Richard Lloyd had been fishing since I left yesterday. He'd blanked.

Friday 11th – Forked Pond

The sweep came and delayed us in our weekly trip to market. But I didn't want to go to market. It'd rained very heavily in the night and I was just itching to get back to Thursley Common. Eventually made it at 3.30pm; much too late. Especially as my pal Bob (Birchett) had arrived minutes before me and dropped into the pads where the carp were cruising. I chatted to him for a while. It was his anniversary and he was hoping to break his season's duck! So I couldn't fish in the corner after all – I'd've been too close to him, even though I was confident I'd get a fish! I tried up in the eastern shallows for a while, where I could see a group of small and medium carp. But only one vague chance. Returning to the corner, I was just in time to see Bob hook a good fish.

I went round to him, took a nice pic of the bent rod, then he lost it! The hook pulled. Had to leave then for a dinner date with Chris Ball and Jan of Yateley.

Sunday 13th – Redmire

Much to my delight I arrived at 6.00pm to find that no one else was there. I'd expected to be the last one in the 'queue', but now I had the place to myself, again. A quick look round rather diminished my optimism. There was no trace of weed and the pool seemed definitely 'older' in the year. Of course, there's no reason why this seasonal barrenness should upset me. In fact it should inspire me. But, after the lush and profuse weedbeds and the days that were very much like the summers of old, this sudden descent towards winter almost made me shiver. There were carp on the bare shallows, though. Only one or two, but enough to encourage a cast.

7.00pm and the sun was already virtually off the water. It glowed on the willows opposite and in the perfect reflections my white quill was almost invisible. I had to squint to see it. I thought I'd better set up before the sudden onrush of night and though I'd decided to fish Ingham's, a glance at the water from the Evening Pitch changed my mind. There were masses of bubbles! I set up two rods and baited with maggot, getting a wretched eel for my trouble. I changed baits and used racing beans. The moon rose and I watched the rooks flying across its face as they settled down for the night. A day from full and very bright. But a thick cloud came across the sky at midnight and lifted the air temperature. Not a twitch, all night. I was only disturbed by the ghost of the boathouse – three times I felt his, her or its presence. No voices this time, just a very curious closeness of presence. I didn't sleep well! (So ended the 29th anniversary of the old '44'.)

Monday 14th

John arrived at 8.00am and we shared a pot of tea while I told him what I'd seen and not seen thus far. The bubbles were going well and I should've really got to work with the maggots instead of trusting to the beans. At 12.30pm John foul-hooked a lovely 21lb mirror from the Ruins. I say 'foul-hooked' as he was using the treacherous 'hair-rig' which, in this book anyway, is tantamount to foul-hooking. It should be seen thus in anyone else's book. But obviously I didn't make a fuss, especially as John had been made so happy by his catch. And at least he still uses old cane carp rods, rather than the plastic stuff. Of course, John, being a modernist, doesn't share my point of view, but as I told Rod earlier in the season when he first enthusiastically described this new method, I felt the 'hair' was an advance too far. It has the potential to make angling so easy as to be meaningless, and with a too-long length of fine line between bait and hook there is also a potential for much genuine foul-hooking. Rod didn't agree; neither does John. I have agreed to differ.

It rained hard. Not a fish appeared on the bleak shallows.

Tuesday 15th

Less bubbling. Still hardly a tweak, and this after a night of torrential rain. If this had been last month, the fish would've been going barmy on the shallows and there would've been numerous chances and opportunities. But, even though it was warmer today, I only saw one bow wave at the top of the pool. Nothing to fish for; all I can do is cast into the grey water and hope. God! I've become conditioned by my summer's stalking. I'd forgotten what it was like to sit behind the blunt-ends of a pair of rods. Did find some fish moving off the dam and float-fished until dark without response. Just before I settled down for the night I had the beginnings of a run but the fish deviously dropped the bait.

Wednesday 16th

Everything looked more cheery today. The mouse who's sharing my bivouac with me was in a perky mood and skipped about for his bread and marmalade. The squirrels were enjoying the acorns, the robin enjoying his song. We went into Ross for lunch and provisions and when we got back I told John that the carp just had to be on the shallows. I even, foolishly, said I'd get one. At least I was right about the first part of my prediction. There weren't many, it's true, but the four double-figure commons and the one of just about 20lbs were the spur I needed to start some proper fishing. Within minutes the largest fish of the bunch was approaching a bunch of maggots that I'd cast into a clear patch between the silkweed, off Wasp Island. He picked up one or two free grubs and came resolutely forward, looking like a certainty for a bit of reel-screaming bow wave. But at the very last inch, when my heart was just about to overtake itself, he turned sharply around and swam off in some sort of dismay, or disgust. I had to laugh, I was so coiled up! In a few minutes, two other carp approached the bait and they too suddenly turned-tail on it and fled. I'm using a size 8 and I can see that, if they're there again tomorrow, I'll have to risk going back to a 12.

From the alder I saw a couple of carp crossing a 'cleaning bowl' a few yards out. It was impossible to cast there from the main island, but I discovered, much to my excitement, that I could wade to the next island – that tiny mound of earth with an ancient and half-dead willow growing from it. Of course there's no room to stand on it, but it's excellent cover to hide behind and gives a tremendous vantage point on what had always been a bit of a 'golden blind spot'. A simple underhand flick had the bait out right in the middle of the smooth depression. The float, set 'long', rode at the edge of the 'saucer'. A carp found the loose maggots I'd tossed in and began to feed. He moved off after a while, but then two fish returned and my float moved once, and then again. My hand hovered over the butt – fancy using that outworn cliché – but I never got a proper chance. And when the fish moved off, they never came back.

From the Island Tree I spotted some very good carp in the margins of the Fence, but by the time I'd moved round there, they'd drifted further out – just beyond range, though they did feed on loose maggots. I went back up to the shallows and something large didn't like the look of my face as I peered round the top willow. It bolted, making a tremendous wave. I didn't even have a rod with me!

Much to my amusement I failed to comply with both my earlier decisions on a new pitch for the night. First it'd been next to the Ash Grove, then the Fence. But here I am in the Stumps! I've set myself up very well. My rods are where I want them, the baits are in the right places, I can even sit up in the dark without bumping my head. And I've got a new bait.

Thursday 17th

Fat lot of good my optimism did me. I cast early and didn't even get a sniff. I scratched around all afternoon on the shallows and though the carp were in evidence and I put my float exactly where I wanted it, they completely failed to appreciate my not inconsiderable efforts.

Around teatime I had a quite remarkable experience. I'd cast my rods back into the deep water between Pitchfords and the Fence and was pleased to see patches of bubbles rising intermittently, right over the baits. As I watched, the bubbling increased and after half an hour the whole area was just a galaxy of carp-bubbles. There couldn't fail to be one fish who wouldn't pick up one bait. I seemed to have the whole population of Redmire within thirty yards of my rod-tips and they were obviously feeding ravenously. But not even a tremor visited my lines. I was, by the end of two hours, quite heartily dispirited.

A heavily banked cloud brought darkness in rapidly. It also brought torrential rain. Then a gale began to blow

133

and I quickly recast the rods and got under canvas for the night.

I sat reading BB by candlelight, warming to his summery tones. The wind crashed into the black poplars above me and the night roared. Rain lashed the bivouac, but the candle only flickered gently. When I'd finished *Confessions* I snuffed the flame and went straight to sleep.

Friday 18th

Woke to a hideous dripping on my head. The roof was leaking! The walls were leaking! The bivvy was like a canvas submarine – perhaps it *was* a canvas submarine: maybe I'd been blown out to sea by the storm and was now residing in the centre-channel. Somehow I managed to position myself between cascades and go back to sleep, where it seemed dry. But the storm had it in for me. It doubled its efforts and, after perhaps an hour, I awoke again, completely soaked. It was trying to get light and I thought my only hope would be to take my creel (somehow still dry) containing tea-making gear etc. and make a run for the pump house. At least I'd be able to enjoy breakfast in comfort. I unzipped the canvas door and was greeted by a most demoralising sight: the butt-end of an Avon rod sticking up out of the margin.

Somehow, I'd forgotten to open the pick-up of the reel and, of course, I had to get the only run of the week on that rod! If only the clutch had been loose – then I'd have heard the scream of it and landed my fish. As it was, I was lucky to still have the rod at all – by good fortune (the only good fortune of the week) the line had caught round the rod-rest as the Avon was dragged forward. That had saved the rod from being hauled into the deepest part of the pool. I reeled in and the lead was still there, the line having parted right down at the hook.

It was a very damp and slightly disconsolate angler who went off down the bank for his breakfast. Then, to cap it all, just after I'd put the kettle on, a joyful John hooked a fish and I had to leave my breakfast to land it for him. It was a superb 24lb mirror, but, unfortunately, on the new diabolic rig (the hook wasn't even in the carp's mouth). I wouldn't use that rig even if I was a starving carp eater and though it sounds like sour grapes it rankled a bit to see a fish caught thus during a blank week. However, I couldn't say anything other than congratulations, as it was a great-looking fish and John was obviously delighted with it. I took a picture of the smiling angler and his catch and then we made a celebratory pot of tea.

After the rain, the sun and I should've been fishing hard then. But, once again, I felt what I've felt before: Redmire had trounced me, had thoroughly defeated me and I couldn't raise my game for a last, wild shot. The sun shone on my float but I was absolutely sure it wouldn't move.

And I laughed. I watched the white clouds sailing across the deep blue sky and thought: how dare I feel despondent! To be here is triumph enough – to be anywhere as beautiful, carp-fishing or not, is something to be gratefully savoured. And what about all those wonderful moments when Redmire was more generous? What about all the giants of the past? Did they count for nothing, just because the fish had eluded me this time? What a joke!

Reasoning thus, half of me suddenly said: 'Aren't you just disguising failure with this waffling philosophy?'. The other half just smiled, and so the battle was won.

Friday 25th – Forked Pond

Had intended to spend the afternoon and evening calming Ellis down before his big exhibition – but then I realised he'd be calm anyway – and the rain looked like holding off and the sun was shining and I hadn't done any work. So I went fishing.

Waded out in the reeds to the edge of the corner lily bed and cast float tackle next to the pads.

A gusting wind made things difficult for a while, but as the sun moved behind the woods the lake calmed so I was able to see what was going on. Big carp were stirring. A fish rolled twice in the pads, a big patch of bubbles rose, the reed clump beneath the rod swayed violently. A carp moved right under the float as I watched through the binoculars – curious, the fact that the slightly trembling quill, distanced somehow through the lens, didn't excite me nearly as much as when seen through the naked eye.

The carp were close. One fish fed eagerly on a scattering of beans and the bubbles speckled the calm water. But the quill never went under and I had to wade out of the swamp before it got too dark to see.

Tuesday 29th – Shillinglee

I'd not intended going anywhere other than Crazyland today as I had some long-standing jobs to deliver. But because I delivered them all, they were all happily accepted *and* I got home sooner than expected, there was just time to slip down for a couple of hours by the water before it got dark.

I'd been thinking about Shillinglee ever since that visit at the start of the month. I'd have preferred a full day's fishing, but the conditions this evening were just right – calm and warm, but with a feel of change in the air. It was nearly 6.00pm by the time I was walking slowly past the boathouse, hoping to see a carp by the old willow. There was no sign of anything there, so I crept along the sweet-smelling reed beds towards the rickety landing stage. Just before I reached it I noticed a dark outspreading cloud of disturbed silt just a few yards out. It could have been caused by a shoal of feeding bream, but a more likely cause was a truffling carp. My rod was already prepared, but I stood still for several minutes, not wanting to make a cast until I got a clearer sight.

The sun was already below the treeline and the light was fading fast, but when something loomed forward out of the mud cloud there was no doubt it was a carp – and a good one. The water was only a yard deep where it swam and I was able to follow its slow course back along the edge of the reeds until it nosed down and started rooting around again. I couldn't believe my luck. I baited a size 8 Mustad with a dozen red maggots and cast a lightly weighted line beyond the feeding fish, inching the bait back until it was close enough. It wasn't necessary to make any free offerings.

Crouching down, I waited impatiently behind a clump of reeds, peering between the stems, hoping the line would draw taut before it was too dark to see. A little patch of bubbles was visible on the surface and I could also see the gentle vortices caused by the carp's tail as it tilted down to feed, but gradually the time ticked by and all details began to merge into the twilight – until, almost astonishingly, I saw exactly what I prayed to see. There was a pale point of light where the slanting line blistered the surface and, as I watched, this little star slid steadily out as the line tightened. Sharply, but not fiercely, I raised the rod and felt a wonderful solidity that only became more solid as the pressure built. Yet there were no fireworks – the carp was just holding its ground as if it couldn't quite work out what had happened. I wound down a yard and put a more extreme bend in the rod, but it had no effect. Was the line snagged round something? No, because finally the fish made a short powerful charge towards the distant willow before turning and boring straight out. I was happy to let it run as far as it wanted that way as the water was clear of any weeds or lilies, but again it didn't go far.

The carp rose up and made a crunching splash, the sound echoing in the silence. A black ripple ringed out across the darkly glowing surface and I took a few paces backwards as the fish wallowed and rolled. It swirled, sloshed and plunged, but didn't take any more line and after a tense few minutes I eased it over the net.

In the half-light it looked magical – an elegant, beautifully formed common that must, I thought, weigh over 20lbs. However, the light was deceiving because when I hoisted the weigh bag on to the scales the pointer stopped at 18lbs 10oz. Statistics aren't important, though, and for the rest of this quiet deep blue evening that carp was the most amazing thing I'd ever seen.

Subscribers

Unbound is a new kind of publishing house. Our books are funded directly by readers. This was a very popular idea during the late eighteenth and early nineteenth centuries. Now we have revived it for the internet age. It allows authors to write the books they really want to write and readers to support the writing they would most like to see published.

The names listed below are of readers who have pledged their support and made this book happen. If you'd like to join them, visit: www.unbound.co.uk.

Paul Bednall
James Bell
Peter Belo
Steven Benger
David Bennett
Jon Berry
Len Betty
Malcolm Beveridge
Ray Bewick & the rest
    of the Bewick Shoal –
    Phil, Claire & Kate
Danny Birch
Stuart Birrell
Clarissa Bishop
Graham Blenkin
Fred Bonney
David Boraston
Martin Bottenheft
Helen Boughton
Jon Boughton
Andrew Bow
Matthew Bowers
Robin Bowker
Kevin Boxall
Binky Bradshaw
Christopher Brass
Lawrence Breakspear
Simon Brogan
Robert Brookes
Gary Brookfield
M. L. Brown
Robert Browne
Bob (Boris) Burchett
Will Burdett
David Burr
Peter Burt
Rob Burt
Xander Cansell
Peter Capps
Phillip Capps
Steve Carden

Graham Carpenter
Paul Carpenter
Andrew Casey
Hugh Caslake
Nigel Causer
River Chapman
David Chesterman
Anthony Chillingworth
Michael Church
Martin Clark
Philip Clark
Andy Clarke
Haydn Clarke
Steve Clements
John Clyde-Evans
Martin Cody
Martin Cole
Sam Coles
Kevin Compton
Daniel Cook
Michael Cook
Paul Cook
Martin Cookson
Andrew Cottier-Cooper
Dean Cox
Tom Craven
Philip Crew
Timothy John Crew
Kelvin Cromwell
Stewart Crowther
Olivia Cryer
Owen Cryer
Wayne Cryer
Glenn Cummins
Steve Curtin
Jon Curtis
Stef Curtis
Roy Daintith
Andy Dalby
Nigel Dale
Jason Dallaway

Monty Dalrymple
Mike Daniel
Les Darlington
Dave Davies
Ken Davies
Rob Davies
Simon Davies
Richard Deacon
The Deaf Cat
Kevin Dean
Gary Dee
John Dine
Luke Dixon
Les Dodd
Richard Donnelly
Mike Donovan
Barry A. Doswell
Andy Doughty
Peter Downing
Emma Drinkall
Paul Drinkall
Anthony R. Dudley
Charlie Duffy
Janet Duncan
Luke Durrant
Simon Dutton
Kevin Dyer
Jeff Edisbury
Andrew Edwards
Lee Edwards
Sian Edwards
Steve Edwards
Jon Elliott
Keith Elliott
Kenny Elton
Nigel Evans
Richard Evans
James Everiss
Nick Fallowfield-Cooper
David Fearn
Mark Fenner

Dave Finch
Barry Fisher
Gordon Fisher
Hannah Fisher
Rob Fletcher
Richard Foley
Brad Ford
David Foreman
Kevin Foster
Peter Foster
Robert Fox
Matt Foyle
Isobel Frankish
Greg Freestone
Alan Frost
Derek Gabb
Mark Gamble
April Gardiner
Ian Garfitt
David Gash
Andy George
Wally Gibb
David Gibson
Keith Gillett
Steve Godwin
Ben Goodman
Jason Goodwin
Vijay Gooriah
Paul Gough
Andy Gray
Richard Gray
Andrew Green
Ivan Greenman
Cliff Greetham
Stephen Grove, Barcelona
Keith 'Gurn' Gurney
Bob Gypps
Darron Hainsworth
Danny Hall
Peter Harbottle
John Harding

Paul Harding
Tom Robert Hardwick
David Harford
Simon Harlond
Peter Harrington
Martin Harrison
Terry Harrison
Nicholas Hart
Paul Hart
Caitlin Harvey
David Hatwell
Andrew Hawkins
John Haynes
Mike Hazzard
James 'shut up' Head
Roger Alan Heaton
Steve Helliwell
Paul Henderson
John Henwood
Phil Hewitson
Jason Hewitt
David Highe
Peter Hill
Mat Hillman
Paul Hiom
Steve Hirst
Graeme Hodges
James Edward Hodkinson
Mark Holt
Alan Hope
Garry Hopkins
James Hore
Bob Hornegold
Neil Hotchin
Kevin Hounsell
Matthew Howell
Brendan Howell & Natalie Goh
David Hudson
Adam Hughes
John Hughes
Peter Hughes

Phil Humm
Jack Hunt
Rod Hutchinson
John Hutton
Edward Ives
David Ivey
Huw James
Andy Jameson
Peter Jaremchuk
Danny Johnson
Jeff Johnson
Mark Johnson
Colwyn Jones
Neil Jones
Nick Jones
Russell Jones
David Kaalstad
Michael Kearney
Ron Kearton
Keebs
Ray Kemp, 'The Colonel',
    Golden Scale Club
Robert Keywood
Dan Kieran
Charles Kirkham
Paul Kitchener
Henrik Korkeamäki
Martin Lamb
Geoff Latham
Jimmy Leach
Stephen Leadbitter
Tony Leggett
Salv Licata
Trevor Lindley
Martyn Lloyd
Jack Loader
Steve Lovegrove
Simon Lovestone
Christopher Lowe
Peter Lundy
Dan Luscombe

SUBSCRIBERS

Robert McClelland
Anthony McGarry
John Mckinven
John McLellan
Craig MacPherson
David Maiden
Anthony Majewski
Robert Major
Daniel Malin
Andy Maple
Andrew Margetson
Richard Masters
John Matthews
Luke Matthews
Stephen Matthews
Phil Mattock
Nigel Maule
David Meek
Tony Meers
James Middleton
Alan Millington
Robert W. Milne
Matthew Minter
Paul Mockridge
Mark Mole
Jim Mooney
Nick J. B. Moore
John Morton
Dick Moss
John Mulcahy
Richard Munday
Steven Murgatroyd
Matthew Murrell
Alfred Nagy
Tony Negueroles
Franklin Newbold
Rob Newman
Graham Nicol
Lee Noakes
Tony Ockendon
Brian OConnor

Jason Oldfield
Steven Oldham
Alan Ong
Erwin Oosterhoff
Frank Oostvogels
Mark Oversby
Gary Packham
Paddex
Julian Palfreyman
Chris Palmer
Jason Palmer
John Palmer
Shaun Parfitt
David Parker
Rob Parker
John Parkinson
David Parman
Kevin Parr
Andrew Partington
Gareth Paul
Daymon Pearcey
Roger Peart
Ettore Pelizzoni
Ian Penny
Mark Penny
Mark Perham
Julie Perkins
Sarah Katie Perkins
Tony Perkins
Rafe Philcox
Gavin Phillips
Kevin Phillips
Adrian Pike
Florence Jean Pike
Laurence Piper
Justine Pirt
Chris Platt
Chris Plumb
Kevin Plummer
Alan Points
Justin Pollard

Mike Pope
Stewart Pope
Ray Potter
Robert Potter
Christian Price
Garry Procter
Ray Pulford
Derek Pye
Chris Quinn
Julie Quinn
Henrik Ragnarsson Stabo
Micah Ramsdale
Jörg Raveling
David Redwood
Stefan Reed
Steven Reed
Colin Reeve
Ian (carpreverend) Regester
Gavin Rendell
Liam Rendell
Rod Rest
Phil Richards
Keith Richardson
River Reads
River Reads Press
Stef Robbelein
Andy Roberts
Eric Roberts
Harry Roberts
John Roberts
Mark Roberts
Nick Roberts
Phill Robinson
Shaun Rock
David Rogers
Scott Rollo
Pete Rose
Tommy Ruffe
Mark Ruggles
Michael Rushforth
Dave Russell

Mark Russell
Piers Russell-Cobb
Robert Ryan
M. Sands
Mark Sarul
George Saul
Anthony Saunders
Mary Searle
Mark Sears
Duncan Seddon
Frank Segrave-Daly
Neil Sharpe
Mark Shaw
Peter Shaw
John Shemmings
Rehman Shivjee
Colin Short
Paul Simpson
Skeff
Norman Skelton
Ian Skinner
Paul Skinner
Andrew Smith
Glenn Smith
Jonathan Smith
Kevin Smith
Michael Smith
Paul Simon Smith
Peter Smith
Steve Smith
Declan Smyth
Paul Snell
Charles Snowden
Kevin Sommerville
Andrew Spencer
Martyn Spencer
Les Spink
Mark Springham
Ian Stacey
George Stannard
Neil Starr

SUBSCRIBERS

Dan Steadman
Dan Stevens
Martin Stevens
Robert Stoker
Andrew Stone
Tony Strongman
Paul Swainson
Craig Swallow
Jonathan Lee Swan
The Sweetcorn Kid
Matthew Tanner
Craig Taylor
David Taylor
Derek Taylor
Matthew Taylor
Neil Taylor
Cristian Teodorescu
Julian Terry
Andy Thacker
Tim Theobald
Ben Thomas
Jason Thomas
Wayne Thomas
Gary Thompson
Adam "One" Toner
Calvin Traynor
James Trimmer
Simon Tubby
Mario Tucci
Stephen Tuck
Jeffrey Tucker
Christian Tyroll
Richard Upton
Steven Uzzell
Ian Vallintine
Hans van der Kleij
Anthony Van Goethem
Jeroen van Wijk
The Vintage Fishing Company
Steven Wadsworth
Nick Wakefield

Ray Badger Walker
Nathan Walter
Isaak Walton
Christopher Ward
Malcolm Ward
Alexander Watson
Stacey E. Weeks
Peter Welford
David Weller
Rod Wells
Peter West
Elliot Enya Louis Wetton
Horace Wetton
Ian Wetton
Michael Wheeler
Peter Whiddett
John White
Philip White
Terry White
John Whitehouse
Grant Whitlock
Dave Whyte
Teresa Wighton
Andy Wilcock
Alan Wilkin
Mark Wilkins
Mark Wilkinson
Jeff Willans
Dean Willders
John Williams
Tim Wilson
Michael Window
Adrian Wood
Derek Wood
Keith Wood
Stephen Wood
Hayley & James Woodhall
Jason Woods
Bill Woodward
Richard Woollard
Daniel Wright

A note about the typeface

The typeface used in this book is a digital representation of Garamond. The original typeface was cut by Parisian publisher and punch-cutter Claude Garamond (c.1480–1561) and shows the influence of types used to print the Aldus Manutius editions of *De Ætna* (1495) and *Hypnerotomachia Poliphili* (1499). Like Mr Yates, Claude was a keen angler with a highly developed constitution, sourcing much of his catch from La Seine, a river whose aquatic inhabitants shared the same health-risks as those who frequented the Thames.

The Garamond typeface has suffered numerous poor interpretations, particularly in the modern age. The version used here is Adobe Garamond Premier Pro designed by Robert Slimbach. Work began on the type in 1989 as part of the Adobe Originals series, and this updated interpretation is closely based on the original sixteenth-century matrices held at the Plantin-Moretus Museum in Antwerp.

Chapter titles are set in Futura Medium, designed in 1927 by German designer Paul Renner. Futura is based on the geometric shapes representative of the Bauhaus design style of the 1920s.